SKILL SHARPENERS
Math 1

Keep Your Child's Academic Skills Sharp

This book belongs to

_____
name

Contents

How to Use This Book 4

Doggy Math (Unit 1) 6

Number & Operations: Write number words; Count objects within 10; Compare numbers within 10; Add within 10

Measurement & Data: Measure length using nonstandard units; Read a graph

Test Your Skills 17

On the Farm (Unit 2) 18

Number & Operations: Count objects within 10; Add and subtract within 10; Use properties of addition (commutative); Solve word problems

Measurement & Data: Interpret a diagram

Geometry: Identify two-dimensional shapes

Test Your Skills 28

Fun with Bears (Unit 3) 29

Number & Operations: Count objects within 10; Add and subtract within 10; Compare numbers within 10; Solve word problems

Measurement & Data: Measure length using inches; Read a graph

Geometry: Identify attributes of shapes

Test Your Skills 40

Creepy Crawlies (Unit 4) 41

Number & Operations: Add and subtract within 10; Use addition and subtraction strategies (addition-subtraction relationship); Solve word problems

Algebra: Identify and extend patterns

Measurement & Data: Tell time to the hour; Represent data on a graph; Read a graph

Test Your Skills 53

On Safari (Unit 5) 54

Number & Operations: Add and subtract within 20; Add three numbers; Use addition and subtraction strategies (counting on, counting back); Solve word problems

Place Value: Count within 100; Count by 10s; Compose numbers with tens and ones

Measurement & Data: Determine the value of coins

Test Your Skills 65

Let's Go Camping (Unit 6) 66

Number & Operations: Add and subtract within 20; Add three numbers; Use addition and subtraction strategies (addition-subtraction relationship, counting on); Solve word problems

Place Value: Count within 100; Count by 10s; Compare two-digit numbers; Compose numbers with tens and ones; Find 10 more or less than a number

Measurement & Data: Read a graph

Test Your Skills 78

Fruity Fun (Unit 7) 79
Number & Operations: Add and subtract within 20; Solve word problems

Place Value: Count by 5s; Compose numbers with tens and ones; Add multiples of 10

Measurement & Data: Represent data on a graph; Read a graph

Geometry: Identify three-dimensional shapes; Identify attributes of shapes

Test Your Skills 90

Chilly Capers (Unit 8) 91
Number & Operations: Add and subtract within 20; Use addition and subtraction strategies (addition-subtraction relationship, doubles); Solve word problems

Place Value: Count by 2s, 5s, and 10s; Add and subtract two-digit numbers; Add and subtract multiples of 10

Measurement & Data: Determine value of coins; Tell time to the half hour; Read a graph

Test Your Skills 103

At the Fair (Unit 9) 104
Number & Operations: Use addition strategies (make 10); Add within 20; Solve word problems

Place Value: Add and subtract two-digit numbers; Add and subtract multiples of 10

Measurement & Data: Measure length using centimeters; Tell time to the half hour

Geometry: Identify equal shares

Test Your Skills 115

Time for Sports (Unit 10) 116
Number & Operations: Add and subtract within 20; Add three numbers; Use addition strategies (regrouping); Solve word problems

Place Value: Count by 5s; Sequence two-digit numbers; Add and subtract two-digit numbers

Measurement & Data: Tell time to the half hour; Read a data table, a tally, and a graph

Test Your Skills 127

Certificate 129
Answer Key 131

How to Use This Book

Practicing Math Skills

Math is in the world around us. Children start to notice how many there are of something when they are quite young, especially if someone else has more! They also notice that quantities change as objects are received, given away, or used. Studies show that children develop math sense and reasoning best through making connections between objects and written numbers. This book will help your child connect real objects and situations with math language and operations.

Use of Manipulatives

Using real-life objects to count, add, or subtract can help young children better understand math concepts. Drawing the objects can also be helpful. As your child completes the activities in this book, provide him or her with objects to use to help work out each math item. Game pieces, silverware, paper clips—any objects around the house will work. Once children become comfortable with counting, adding, and subtracting, they will probably no longer need the real-life objects to help them calculate.

Counting, Adding, and Subtracting Activities

Provide support as your child works through counting, addition, and subtraction items. Read the directions to your child. If there is an example at the top of the page, explain it to your child. Next, to verify understanding, have your child explain the example to you. Point to any math symbols on the page and ask your child what they mean. Explain any math symbols that your child is not sure of. If your child struggles with problems that are not illustrated, have your child draw, use manipulatives, or act out the problem.

Word Problems

Word problems help relate math to real-life situations and develop reasoning skills. Read the word problem to your child if needed and make sure he or she understands all the words. Encourage your child to draw the situation; provide objects to represent the quantities. Give your child a chance to figure out the problem before you offer help. If your child is stuck or unsure how to proceed, use guiding questions such as, "What is the goal of the problem? What information do you have already? What do these numbers have to do with each other? Do you think you should add or subtract? Is there another number you need to figure out before you can find the answer?"

Other Math Skills

Numbers are used to make graphs and measurements. Geometric shapes are explored and used to make patterns. Skip-counting creates dot-to-dot pictures. Different representations of time and money are matched. For these and other activities, read the directions to your child and make sure he or she understands the vocabulary. Allow enough time for your child to solve the problem or complete the task. If he or she is unable to, suggest strategies to try or provide other support.

Number Words

Skills:
Write number words; Count objects within 10

Write each number word.

0	1	2	3	4	5
zero	one	two	three	four	five
6	7	8	9	10	
six	seven	eight	nine	ten	

3 _____   2 _____   1 _____

10 _____   9 _____   6 _____

0 _____   4 _____   5 _____

7 _____   8 _____

Count. Draw a line to match.

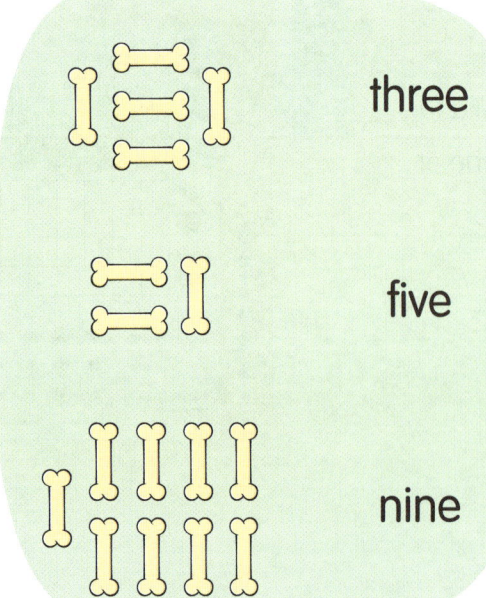

three

five

nine

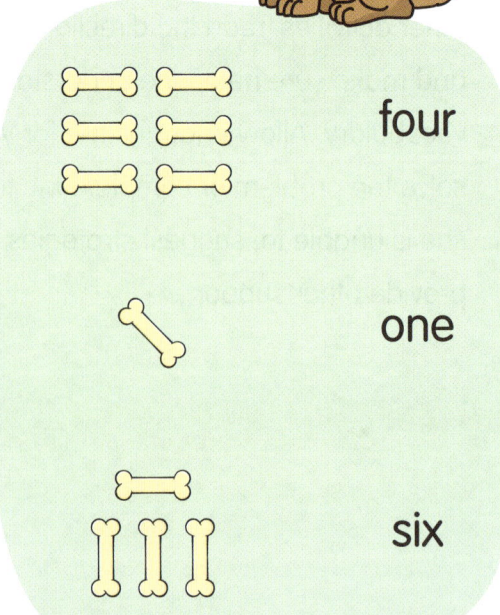

four

one

six

Doggy Math

6

Skill Sharpeners: Math • EMC 8251 • © Evan-Moor Corp.

Cute Pups

Count the dogs. Circle the number.

Find the Doghouse

Skill: Count objects within 10

Count. Draw lines to match the dogs to their houses.

Doggy Bones

Circle 7 bones.

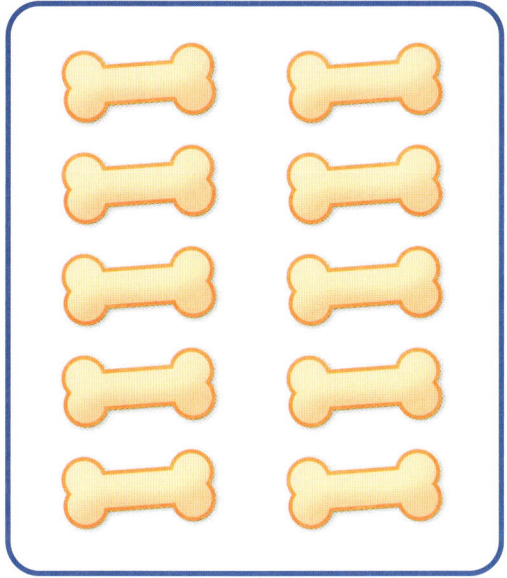

Circle 9 bones.

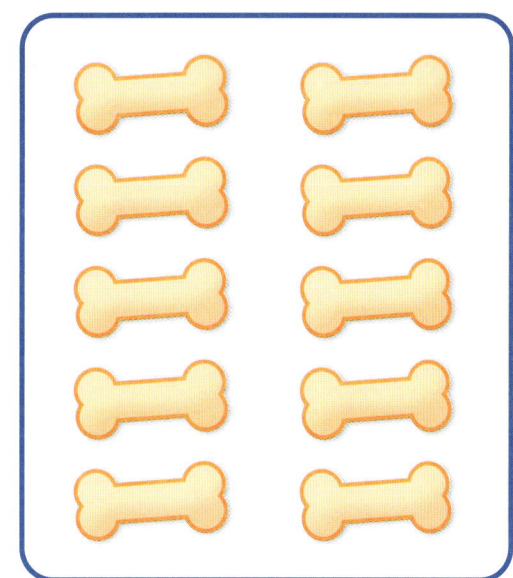

Draw 8 bones.

Draw 10 bones.

Circle the larger number on each bone.

Skills:
Count objects within 10; Compare numbers within 10

Count and Tell

Skills:
Count objects within 10; Compare numbers within 10

How many legs?  _____ has _____ legs.

How many ears?  _____ has _____ ears.

How many feet in all?  and  have _____ feet in all.

How many bones?  _____ has _____ bones.

Which answer is the largest? _____

Which answer is the smallest? _____

More or Less

Skills: Count objects within 10; Compare numbers within 10

Write the numbers. Then circle the set with **more**.

Write the numbers. Then circle the set with **less**.

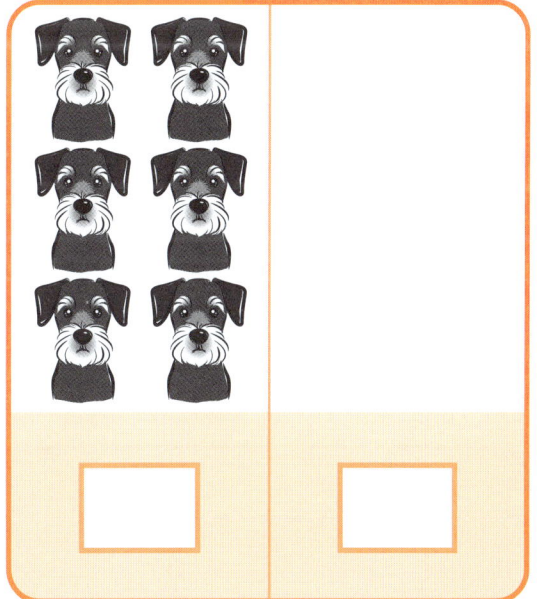

Which number is larger?

| 5 or 8 | 3 or 1 |

Which number is smaller?

| 7 or 2 | 9 or 0 |

Doggy Math

Making 6

Skill: Add within 10

Write the numbers that show different ways you can make 6.

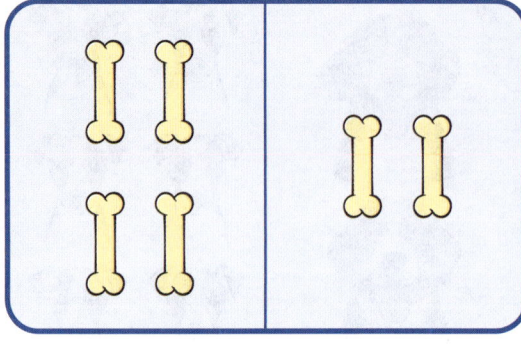 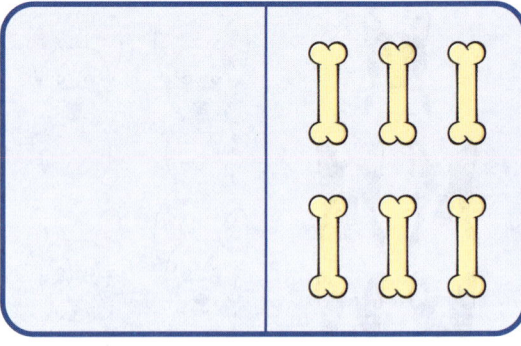

__4__ and __2__ ____ and ____

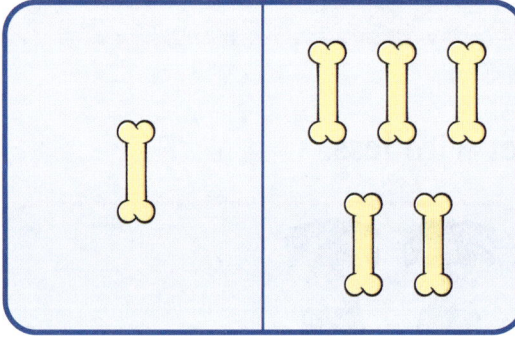 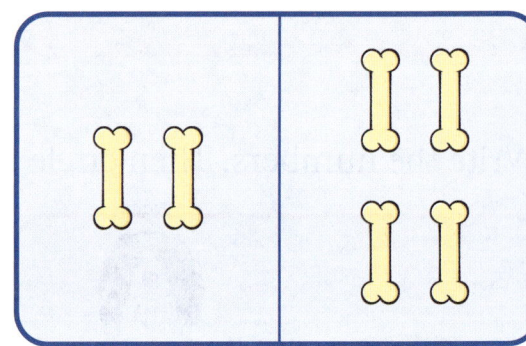

____ and ____ ____ and ____

Draw bones to show two other ways you can make 6.

 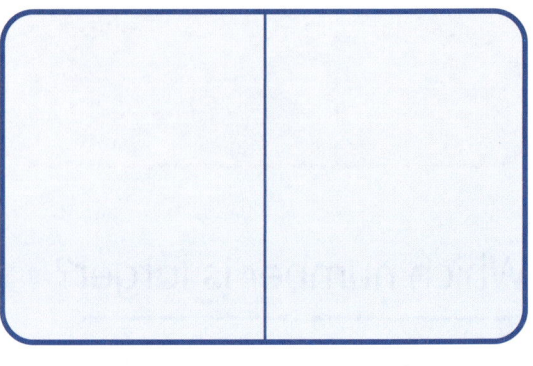

____ and ____ ____ and ____

Making 7

Draw the cans you need to make 7. Write the numbers.

__5__ and __2__　　　　　____ and ____

____ and ____　　　　　____ and ____

____ and ____　　　　　____ and ____

Making 8

Skill: Add within 10

Write the numbers that show different ways you can make 8.

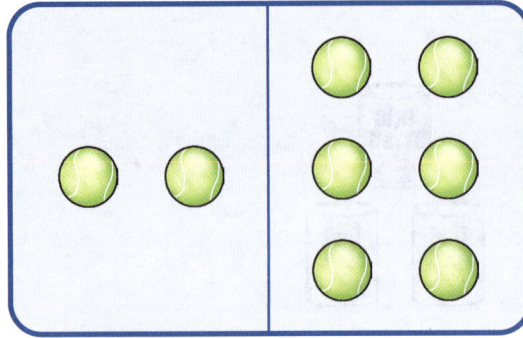   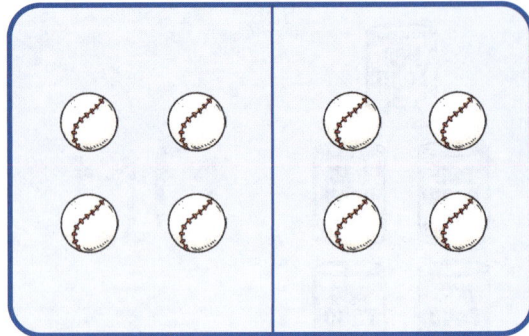

_____ and _____   _____ and _____

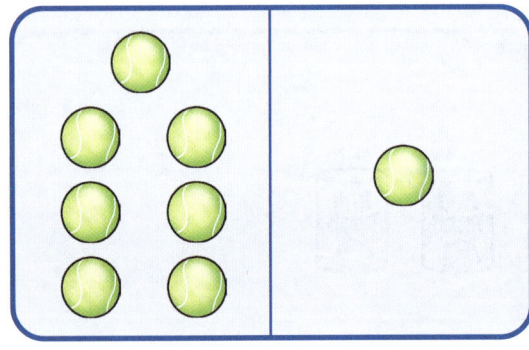   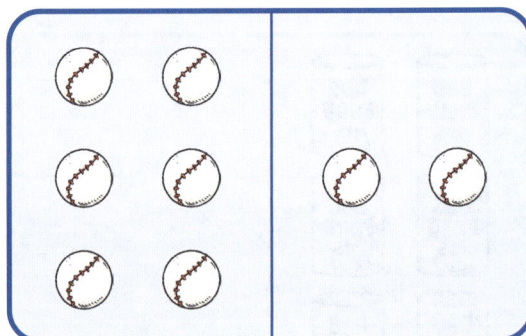

_____ and _____   _____ and _____

Draw bones to show two other ways you can make 8.

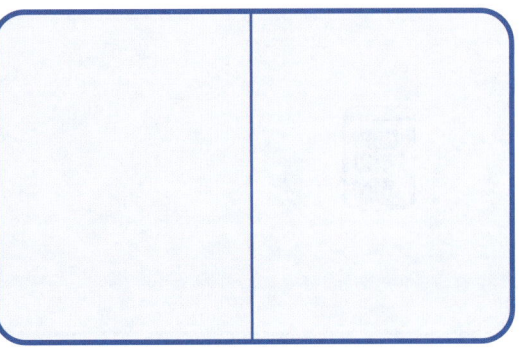   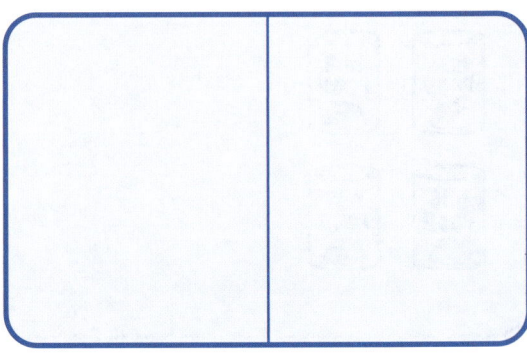

_____ and _____   _____ and _____

Dog Bone Measuring

Skill: Measure length using nonstandard units

How long is each object?

_____

_____

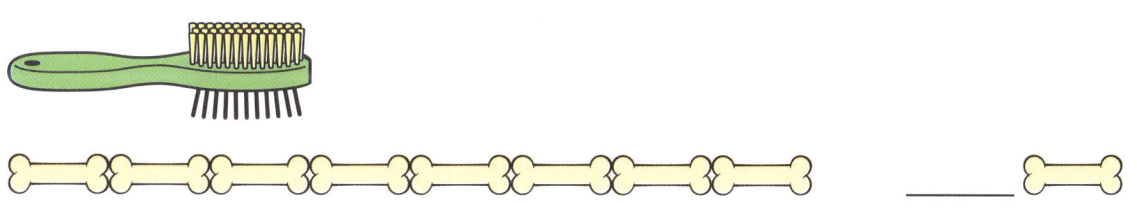
_____

_____

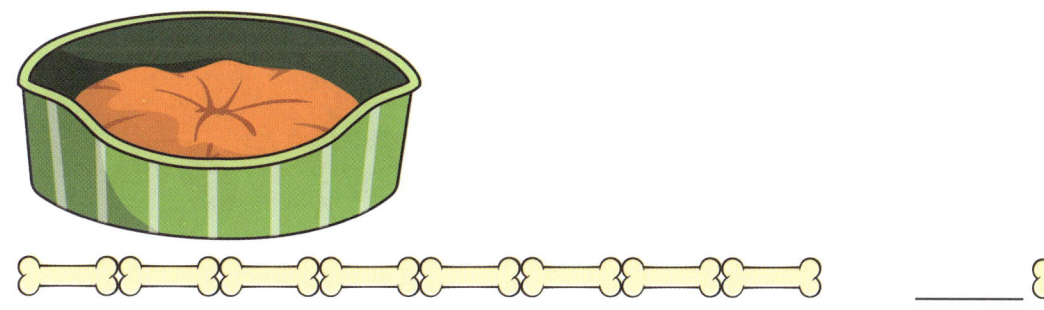
_____

The Pet Store

Skill: Read a graph

Read the graph about a pet store. Answer the questions.

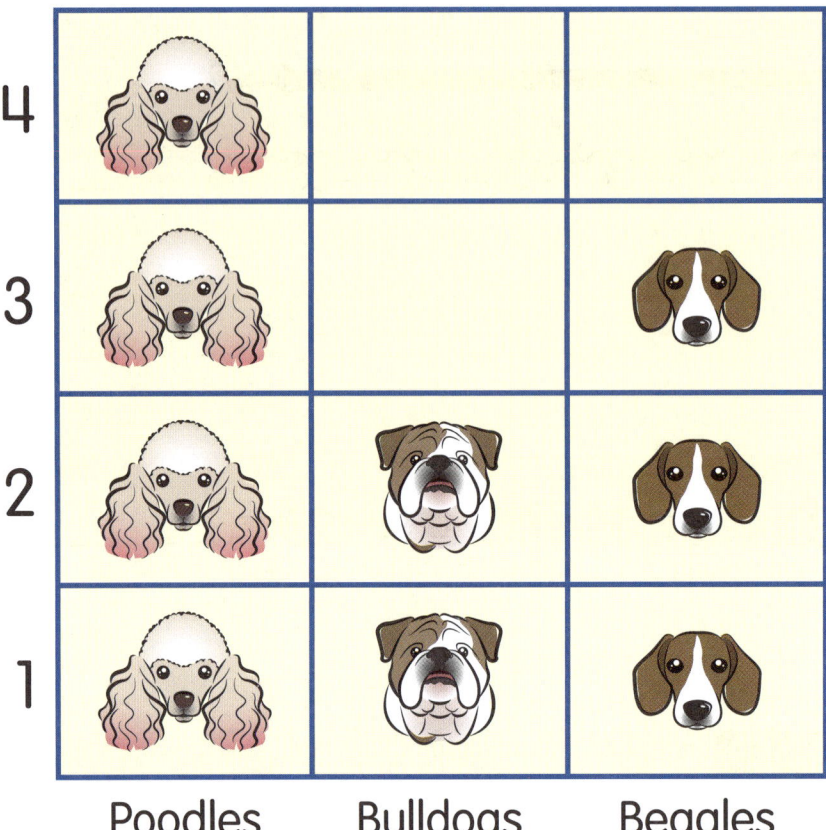

How many dogs are in the store?

How many dogs in all? _____

Are there more  or  ?

The store has the most    .

Count the dogs. Write the number to tell how many.

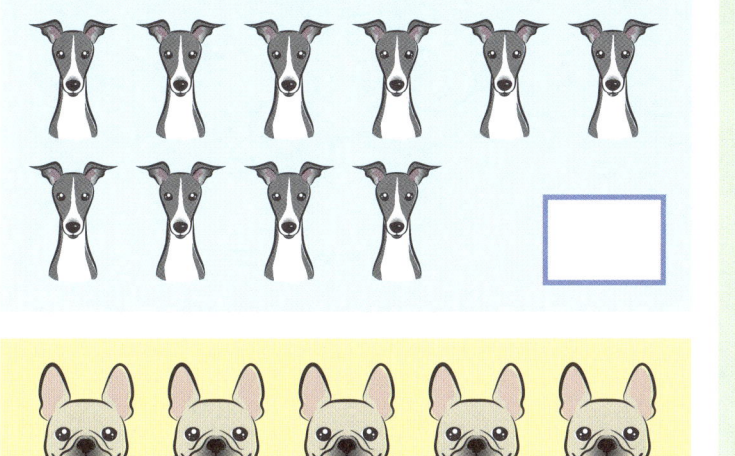

Fill in the circle to show how long it is.

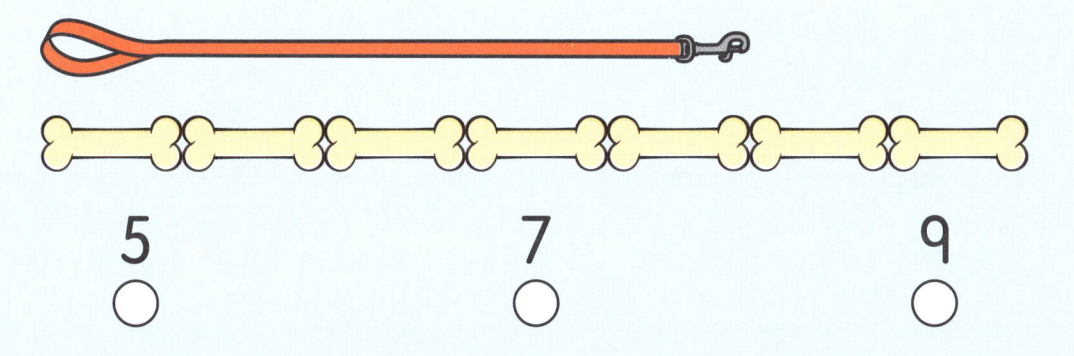

5   7   9
○   ○   ○

Draw the cans you need to make 8. Write the numbers.

_____ and _____

Doggy Math

Let's Add Sheep

Add.

1 + 2 = ___

3 + 1 = ___

1 + 4 = ___

6 + 0 = ___

Write and add.

_1_ + _1_ = _2_

___ + ___ = ___

___ + ___ = ___

___ + ___ = ___

Animals on the Farm

Note: You may need to help your child read the word problems.

Skills:
Solve word problems; Add within 10

Add.

There are 2 horses.
2 more horses come.
How many horses now?

__2__ + __2__ = __4__

[4] horses

There are 3 sheep.
3 more sheep come.
How many sheep now?

___ + ___ = ___

[ ] sheep

There are 0 hens.
5 hens come.
How many hens now?

___ + ___ = ___

[ ] hens

There are 2 goats.
1 more goat comes.
How many goats now?

___ + ___ = ___

[ ] goats

On the Farm

Playful Sheep

Add.

2 + 2 = ___   3 + 2 = ___   4 + 2 = ___

1 + 2 = ___   0 + 2 = ___   1 + 1 = ___

3 + 1 = ___   1 + 0 = ___   0 + 3 = ___

0 + 0 = ___   2 + 3 = ___   3 + 3 = ___

```
  3      2      0      3      0
+ 1    + 3    + 3    + 3    + 0
□      □      □      □      □

  1      4      4      2      1
+ 0    + 2    + 1    + 2    + 1
□      □      □      □      □
```

Skill: Add within 10

The Answer Is the Same

Skill: Use properties of addition (commutative)

Add.

3 + 2 = ___	0 + 1 = ___	1 + 2 = ___
2 + 3 = ___	1 + 0 = ___	2 + 1 = ___
0 + 4 = ___	1 + 5 = ___	0 + 6 = ___
4 + 0 = ___	5 + 1 = ___	6 + 0 = ___
3 + 0 = ___	3 + 1 = ___	4 + 2 = ___
0 + 3 = ___	1 + 3 = ___	2 + 4 = ___

Write two addition problems for each cow.

EXAMPLE

1, 2, 3

_1_ + _2_ = _3_

_2_ + _1_ = _3_

2, 3, 5   1, 5, 6

___ + ___ = ___   ___ + ___ = ___

___ + ___ = ___   ___ + ___ = ___

On the Farm

How Many Chicks?

Skill: Subtract within 10

Subtract.

3 − 2 = __1__   5 − 3 = ____

4 − 0 = ____   6 − 4 = ____

Write and subtract.

__5__ − __1__ = __4__   ____ − ____ = ____

____ − ____ = ____   ____ − ____ = ____

Note: You may need to help your child read the word problems.

Animals Go Away

Skills:
Solve word problems;
Subtract within 10

Subtract.

There are 5 hens.
1 hen goes away.
How many hens now?

____ − ____ = ____

☐ hens

There are 4 cows.
2 cows go away.
How many cows now?

____ − ____ = ____

☐ cows

There are 6 chicks.
2 chicks go away.
How many chicks now?

____ − ____ = ____

☐ chicks

There are 5 horses.
3 horses go away.
How many horses now?

____ − ____ = ____

☐ horses

On the Farm

Swim Time

Skill: Subtract within 10

Subtract.

5 − 5 = ___   2 − 1 = ___   6 − 5 = ___

3 − 1 = ___   0 − 0 = ___   4 − 3 = ___

6 − 6 = ___   5 − 2 = ___   3 − 0 = ___

5 − 0 = ___   6 − 2 = ___   1 − 1 = ___

5	2	4	5	1
−5	−1	−3	−5	−0
☐	☐	☐	☐	☐

6	5	3	5	3
−3	−2	−0	−4	−1
☐	☐	☐	☐	☐

On the Farm

Farmer Mac's House

Skill: Identify two-dimensional shapes

Color the shapes.

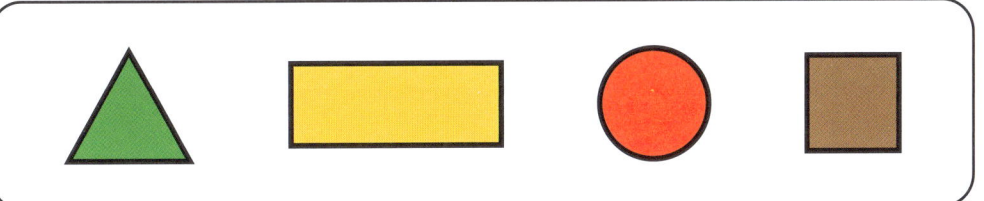

Count each shape. Write how many.

_____   _____   _____   _____

Look Both Ways

Skill: Identify two-dimensional shapes

Solve the riddle. Write the matching letter above the shape.

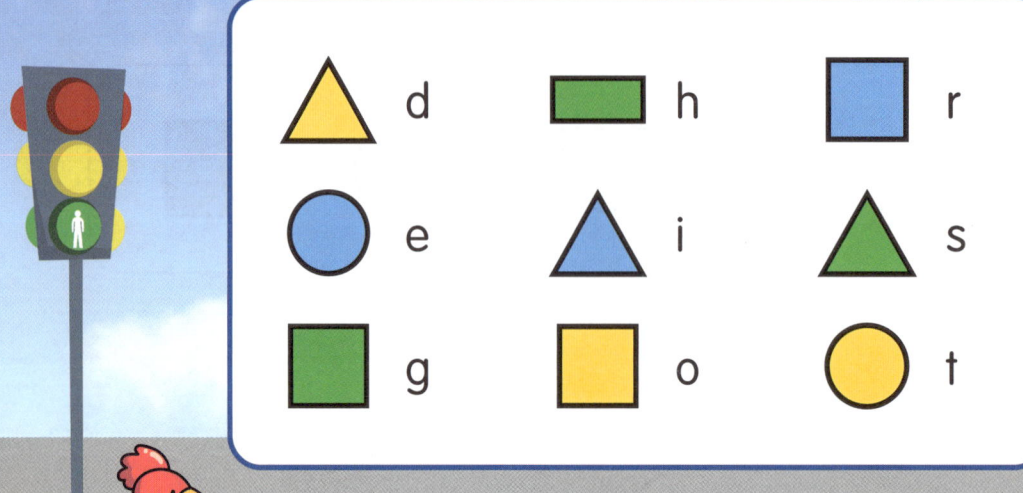

Why did the chicken cross the road?

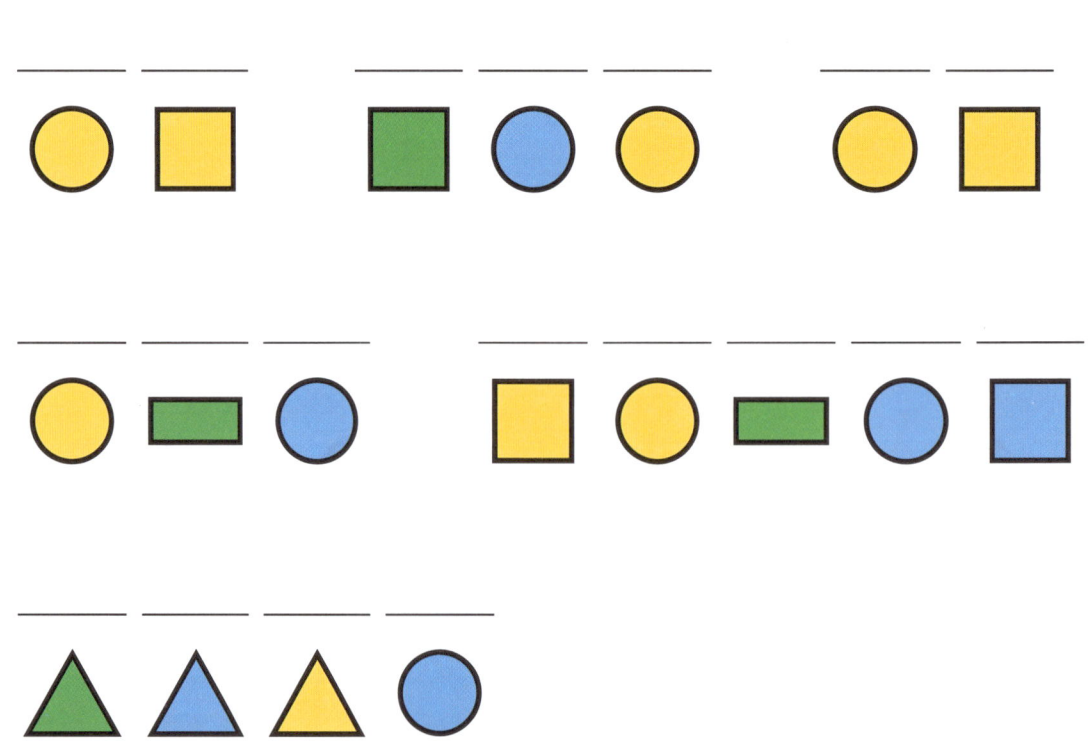

Chicks and Hens

Skills: Count objects within 10; Interpret a diagram

Write how many.

 in the ◯ ? _____

 in the ☐ ? _____

 in both the ◯ and the ☐ ? _____

 in both the ◯ and the ☐ ? _____

 in the ☐ but **not** in the ◯ ? _____

On the Farm

Add.

3 + 3 = ___   1 + 2 = ___   2 + 3 = ___

Subtract.

4 – 1 = ___   6 – 2 = ___   6 – 6 = ___

Color the shapes.

Read and answer.

There are 3 🐸 in the mud. 2 more 🐸 come.

How many 🐸 are in the mud now?   ___

How Many Bears?

Skill: Add within 10

Add.

7 + 1 = ____

3 + 4 = ____

1 + 6 = ____

5 + 3 = ____

Write and add.

____ + ____ = ____

____ + ____ = ____

____ + ____ = ____

____ + ____ = ____

Teddy Bear Colors

Note: You may need to help your child read the word problems.

Skills: Solve word problems; Add within 10

Add.

4 bears are brown.
4 bears are white.
How many bears in all?

___ + ___ = ___

☐ bears

2 bears are red.
4 bears are blue.
How many bears in all?

___ + ___ = ___

☐ bears

6 bears are green.
2 bears are yellow.
How many bears in all?

___ + ___ = ___

☐ bears

4 bears are purple.
3 bears are orange.
How many bears in all?

___ + ___ = ___

☐ bears

Fun with Bears

Skill Sharpeners: Math • EMC 8251 • © Evan-Moor Corp.

Hungry Bears

Note: You may need to help your child read the word problems.

Skills:
Solve word problems;
Subtract within 10

Read. Write the problems. Solve them.

Black Bear had 7 berries. He ate 3 berries.

How many berries were left?

$$\begin{array}{r} 7 \\ -\ 3 \\ \hline 4 \end{array}$$

__4__ berries were left.

6 baby bears were in a tree. 1 climbed down.

How many baby bears were still in the tree?

_____ baby bears were still in the tree.

Grizzly Bear caught 8 fish. 1 swam away.

How many fish were left?

_____ fish were left.

Sun Bear had 7 nuts. Sun Bear ate 5 of them.

How many nuts were left?

_____ nuts were left.

Fun with Bears

Color the Bear

Subtract. Color.

orange 0   brown 1   blue 2   red 3

green 4   purple 5   yellow 6

Subtract.

6 − 6 = ___   3 − 3 = ___   4 − 4 = ___

8 − 8 = ___   5 − 5 = ___   2 − 2 = ___

When you subtract a number from itself, you get ___.

Skill: Subtract within 10

Fun with Bears

Bears at Play

Skill: Add and subtract within 10

Add.

2 + 3 = ___   4 + 4 = ___   6 + 1 = ___

4 + 2 = ___   2 + 5 = ___   5 + 3 = ___

Subtract.

6 − 6 = ___   8 − 1 = ___   7 − 5 = ___

5 − 3 = ___   7 − 3 = ___   8 − 2 = ___

Add or subtract.

3	6	5	4	2
+3	+2	+0	+3	+6
☐	☐	☐	☐	☐

6	7	8	5	8
−2	−1	−8	−2	−6
☐	☐	☐	☐	☐

In the Woods

Skill: Measure length using inches

How many inches?

The berry is _____ inch wide.

The hive is _____ inches wide.

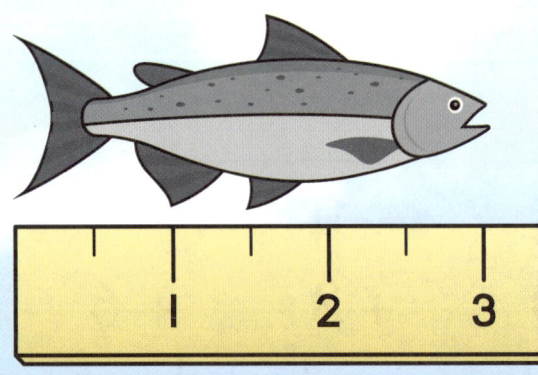

The fish is _____ inches long.

The flower is _____ inch wide.

The baby bear is _____ inches long.

Bear Watching

Read the graph. Answer the questions.

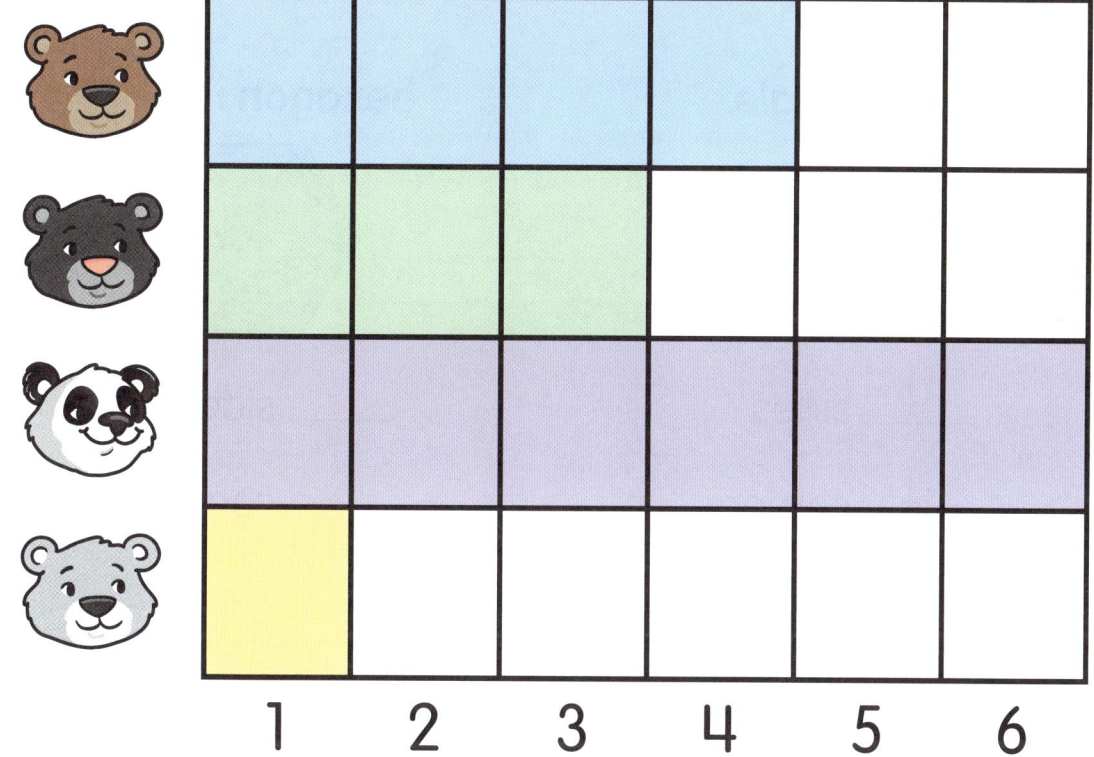

How many ? _____

How many ? _____

How many more  than ? _____ more

How many more  than ? _____ more

How many more  than ? _____ more

Corners and Sides

Skill: Identify attributes of shapes

Count the number of sides and corners. Write the numbers.

rectangle

_4_ sides
_4_ corners

hexagon
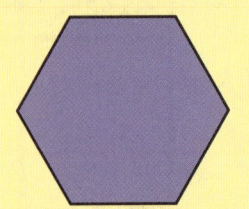
____ sides
____ corners

pentagon

____ sides
____ corners

circle
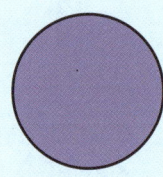
____ sides
____ corners

square
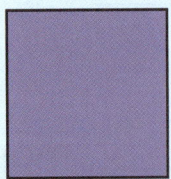
____ sides
____ corners

triangle
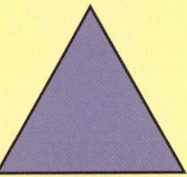
____ sides
____ corners

I Can Draw Shapes!

Skill: Identify attributes of shapes

Read how many sides and corners.
Draw the shapes.

4 sides 4 corners	3 sides 3 corners
4 equal sides 4 corners	0 sides 0 corners

Write to answer the questions.

How are a ▢ and a ▬ alike?

_____

How are a ▢ and a ▬ different?

_____

Fun with Bears

39

Write > or < to show **greater than** or **less than**.

4 ◯ 7   6 ◯ 5

Fill in the circle for the answer.

4 + 4 =   6 ◯   7 ◯   8 ◯

6 + 2 =   6 ◯   7 ◯   8 ◯

8 − 3 =   3 ◯   4 ◯   5 ◯

7 − 4 =   3 ◯   4 ◯   5 ◯

Count the sides and corners.

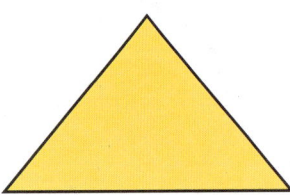

_____ sides

_____ corners

How Many Butterflies?

Add.

$$\begin{array}{r} 4 \\ +3 \\ \hline \square \end{array}$$

$$\begin{array}{r} 5 \\ +4 \\ \hline \square \end{array}$$

$$\begin{array}{r} 8 \\ +0 \\ \hline \square \end{array}$$

$$\begin{array}{r} 3 \\ +6 \\ \hline \square \end{array}$$

Subtract.

$$\begin{array}{r} 7 \\ -7 \\ \hline \square \end{array}$$

$$\begin{array}{r} 9 \\ -2 \\ \hline \square \end{array}$$

$$\begin{array}{r} 9 \\ -3 \\ \hline \square \end{array}$$

$$\begin{array}{r} 8 \\ -5 \\ \hline \square \end{array}$$

Skill: Add and subtract within 10

Creepy Crawlies

Bug Problems

Note: You may need to help your child read the word problems.

Read. Write the problems. Solve them.

---

8 🐜 were marching. 3 stopped.

How many ants were still marching?

_____ ants were still marching.

---

4 🐞 were looking for food. 3 more came.

How many ladybugs were there in all?

There were _____ ladybugs in all.

---

7 🦗 were hopping. 2 more came.

How many crickets were hopping then?

_____ crickets were hopping then.

---

9 🐝 were buzzing. 4 stopped.

How many bees were still buzzing?

_____ bees were still buzzing.

Skills: Solve word problems; Add and subtract within 10

Creepy Crawlies

Busy Ants

Skills: Add and subtract within 10; Use addition and subtraction strategies (addition-subtraction relationship)

Write two addition problems and two subtraction problems.

6 + 3 = 9

3 + 6 = 9

9 − 3 = 6

9 − 6 = 3

___ − ___ = ___

___ − ___ = ___

___ + ___ = ___

___ + ___ = ___

___ + ___ = ___

___ + ___ = ___

___ − ___ = ___

___ − ___ = ___

___ − ___ = ___

___ − ___ = ___

___ + ___ = ___

___ + ___ = ___

Mark ☒ the one that does **not** belong in the family of facts.

1 + 7 = 8   7 + 1 = 8   8 − 1 = 7   7 − 1 = 6

☐   ☐   ☐   ☐

Write the missing fact from this family.

___ − ___ = ___

What's Missing?

Write the numbers.

2 + 8 = ___

7 + ___ = 7

4 + ___ = 8

1 + ___ = 9

9 − ___ = 5

8 − ___ = 0

6 − ___ = 4

9 − 6 = ___

4 + 6 = ___

Creepy Crawlies

Make Ten

Skill: Add within 10

Draw circles to make 10. Then write an addition sentence.

EXAMPLE

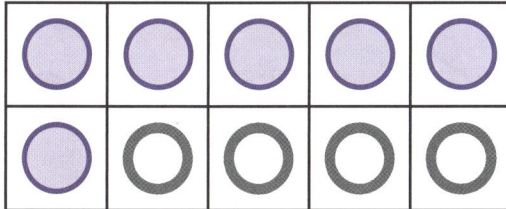 

6 + 4 = 10

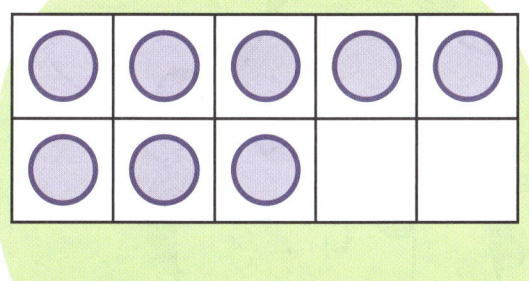 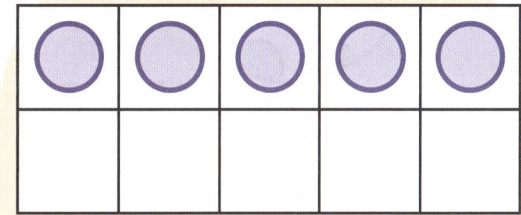

_____ _____

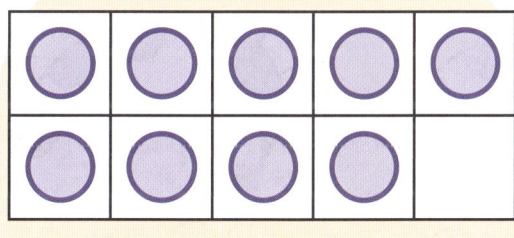 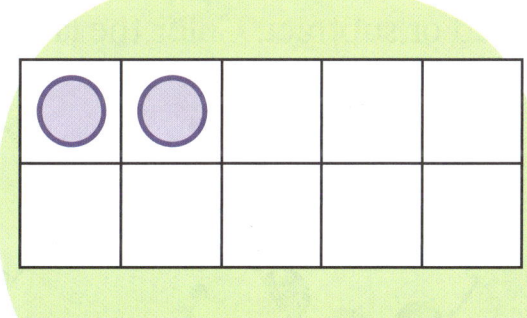

_____ _____

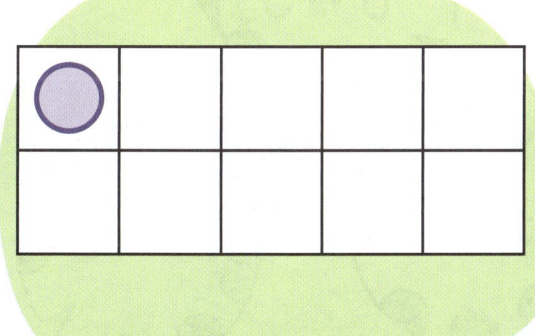 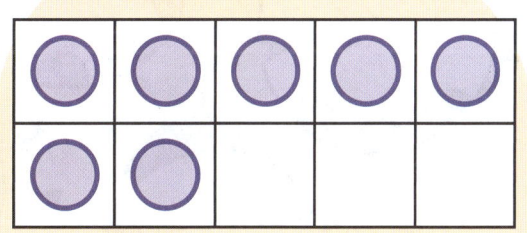

_____ _____

Creepy Crawlies

Ladybugs Are Everywhere!

Skill: Add and subtract within 10

Add or subtract. Color the ladybugs that = 6.

Add or subtract. Color the ladybugs that = 7.

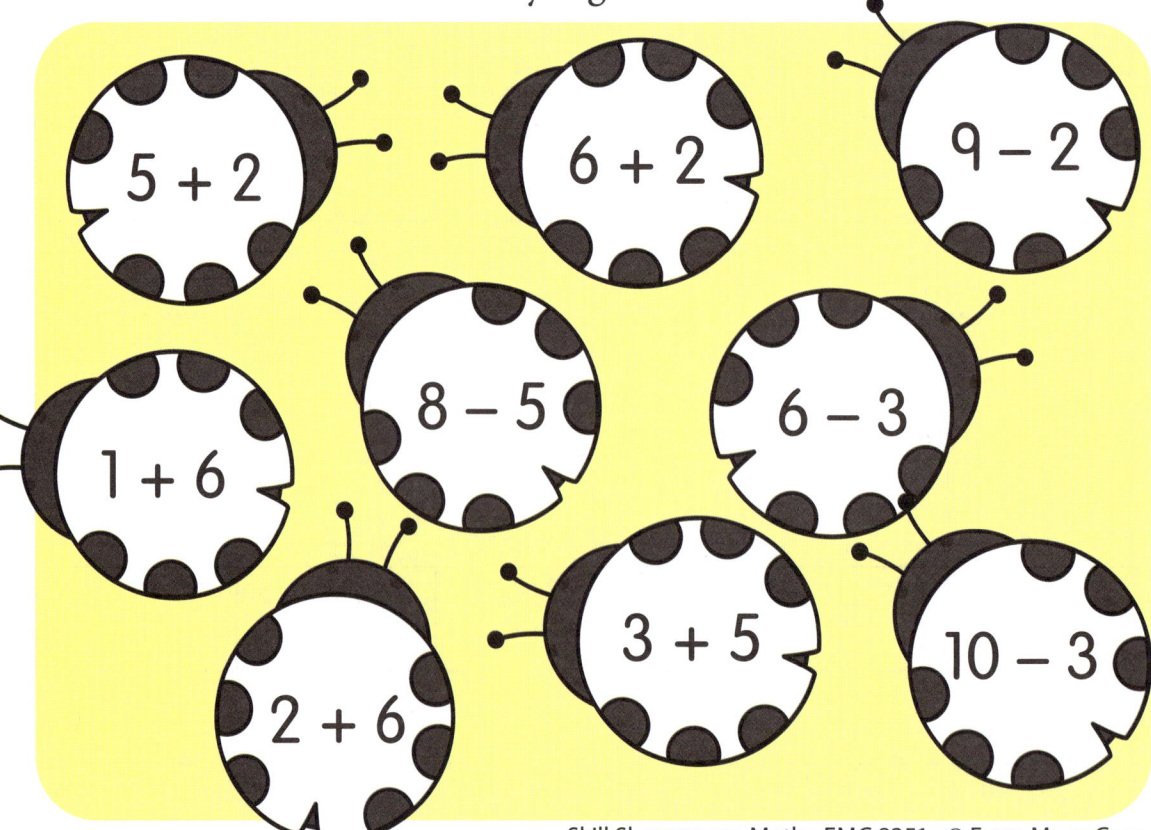

Note: You may need to help your child read the word problems.

Bug Stories

Read. Write the problems. Solve them.

9  were crawling. 3 stopped to take a nap.

How many snails were still crawling?

_____ snails were still crawling.

5  were flying. 3 more dragonflies came.

How many dragonflies were flying then?

_____ dragonflies were flying then.

6  were eating grass. All 6 hopped away.

How many grasshoppers were still eating grass?

_____ grasshoppers were still eating grass.

6  were sipping nectar. 4 more butterflies came.

How many butterflies were sipping nectar then?

_____ butterflies were sipping nectar then.

Skills:
Solve word problems; Add and subtract within 10

Creepy Crawlies

Garden Friends

Look at the grass. Count how many.
Color the graph to show how many.

There are the most

There are the least

Which 2 have the same number?

Skills:
Represent data on a graph;
Read a graph

Pretty Patterns

Circle the shape that comes next in each pattern.
Then label the pattern.

EXAMPLE

A A B A A B A

Hungry Caterpillars

Skill: Add and subtract within 10

Find the answers. Draw a line from each 🐛 to the 🌼 with the correct answer.

Draw a picture to show each number sentence. Write the answer.

| $5 + 5 = \_\_\_$ | $9 - 7 = \_\_\_$ | $3 + 6 = \_\_\_$ |

Counting Back

Skill: Use subtraction strategies (counting back)

You can **count back** to subtract small numbers such as 1, 2, and 3.

EXAMPLE

8 − 2 = ?

Start with the first number. It's 8.
Count back 2 more numbers.
You get 8   7   6.

The answer is 6!

10 − 3 = ____

10 − 2 = ____

8 − 1 = ____

9 − 2 = ____

10 − 1 = ____

9 − 1 = ____

11 − 3 = ____

12 − 3 = ____

11 − 2 = ____

9 − 3 = ____

Write two more problems you can solve by counting back.

____ − ____ = ____   ____ − ____ = ____

On Safari

Safari Animals

Note: You may need to help your child read the word problems.

Skills: Add and subtract within 20; Solve word problems

Read. Write the problems. Solve them.

6 zebras were playing. 5 more zebras came to play. How many zebras were playing then?

__6__ + __5__ = __11__

[11] zebras were playing then.

12 elephants were eating. 3 elephants went away. How many elephants were left?

____ – ____ = ____

[ ] elephants were left.

11 lions were sleeping. Then 3 lions woke up. How many lions were still sleeping?

____ – ____ = ____

[ ] lions were still sleeping.

8 ostriches were running. 4 more ostriches joined them. How many ostriches were running then?

____ + ____ = ____

[ ] ostriches were running then.

Count to 100

Write the numbers **1** to **100** in order.

1									
11									
21									
31									
41									
51									
61									
71									
81									
91									

Skill: Count within 100

Who Is It?

Skill: Count by 10s

Count by 10s. Then write the numbers.

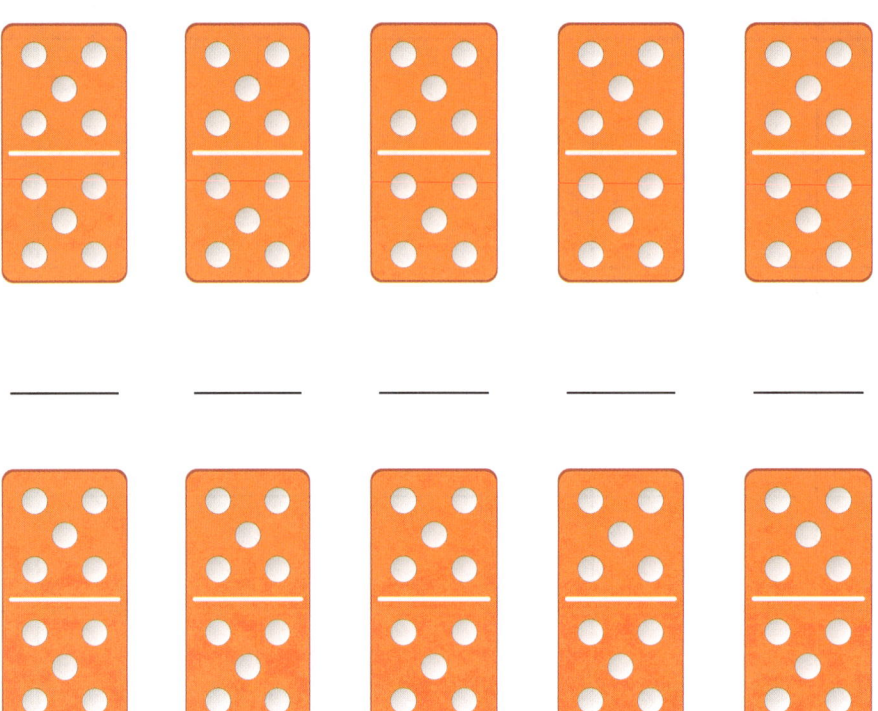

___ ___ ___ ___ ___

___ ___ ___ ___ ___

Connect the dots. Start at 10.

Add Three Numbers

Skill: Add three numbers

How many?

EXAMPLE

3
1
+4
[8]

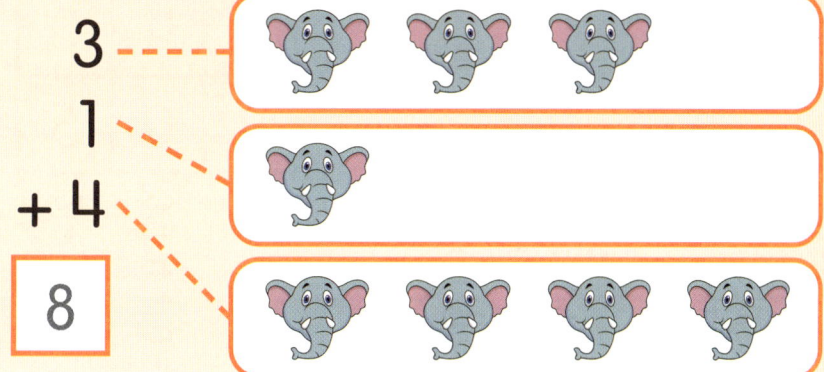

2	3	6	4	8
3	5	1	3	0
+4	+1	+2	+1	+2
☐	☐	☐	☐	☐

1	1	2	3	4
7	6	5	4	3
+1	+3	+2	+3	+2
☐	☐	☐	☐	☐

5	6	3	5	7
2	2	4	2	0
+3	+1	+2	+1	+2
☐	☐	☐	☐	☐

On Safari

Mystery Boxes

Skill: Add three numbers

Write the missing numbers.

EXAMPLE

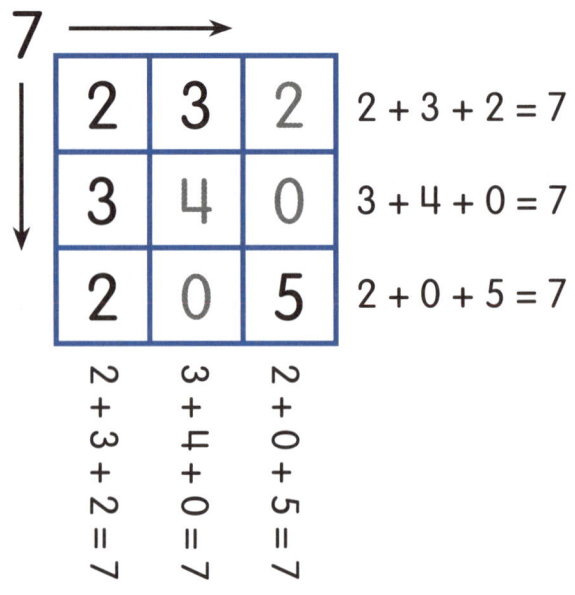

8 →
	2	3
	5	
3		

9 →
	3	4
		2
5	1	

10 →
	3	
4		2
	3	3

On Safari

60

Skill Sharpeners: Math • EMC 8251 • © Evan-Moor Corp.

Make Tens and Ones

Circle groups of 10 animals.
How many tens and ones are there?

Skill: Compose numbers with tens and ones

EXAMPLE

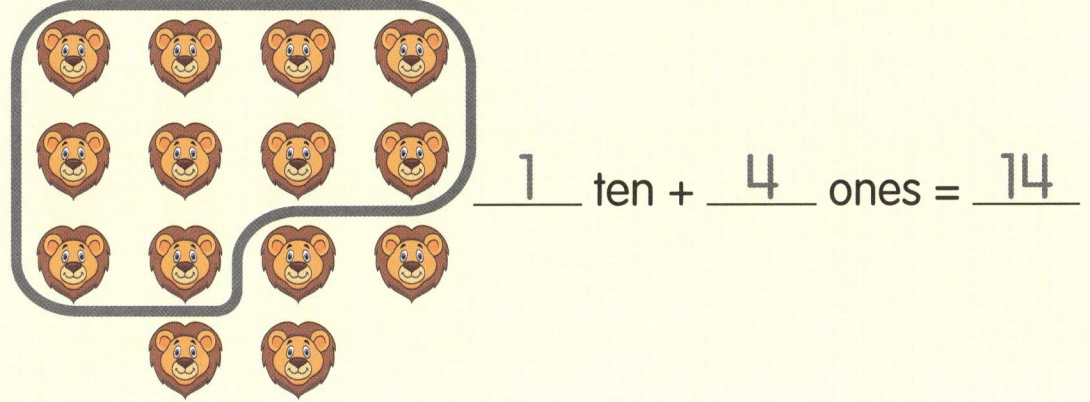

___1___ ten + ___4___ ones = ___14___

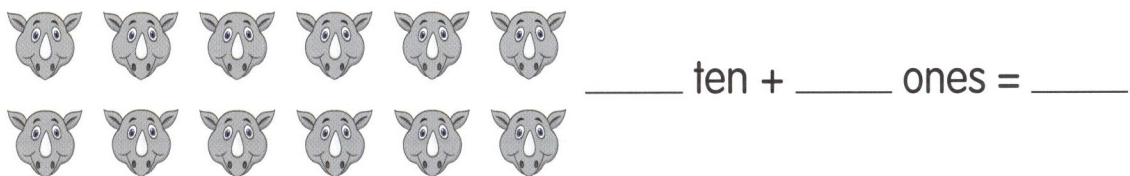

_____ ten + _____ ones = _____

_____ ten + _____ ones = _____

_____ ten + _____ ones = _____

_____ tens + _____ ones = _____

On Safari

Tens and Ones

Skill:
Compose numbers with tens and ones

Each block is one.
Here are **3 ones**.

There are 10 blocks in this set. This is **1 ten**.

How many?

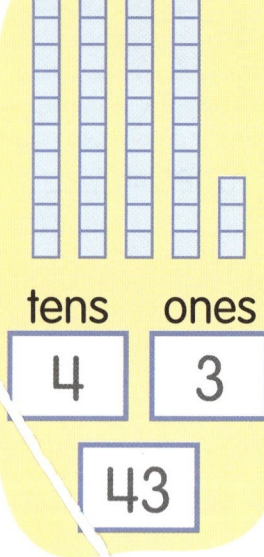

tens	ones
4	3

43

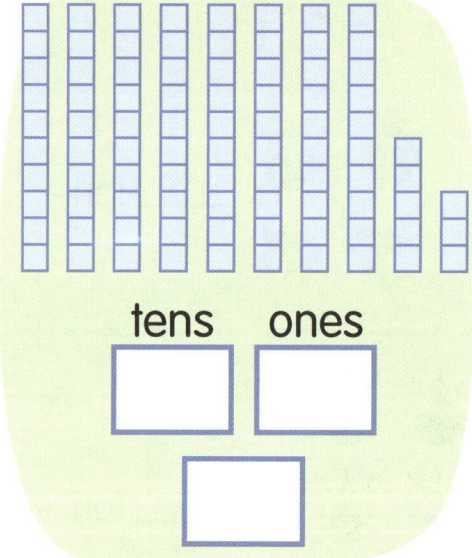

tens   ones

tens   ones

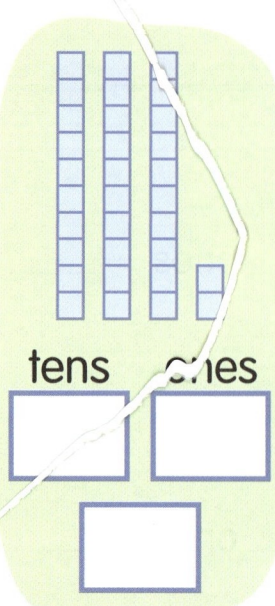

tens   ones

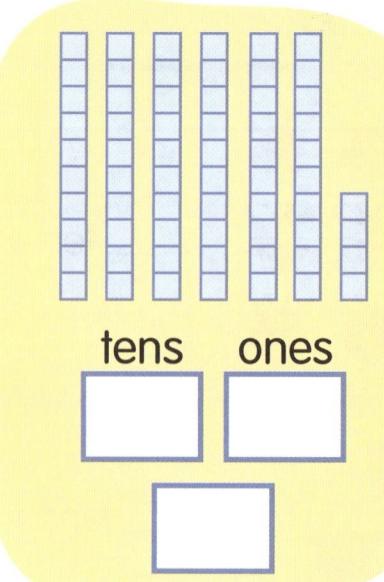

tens   ones

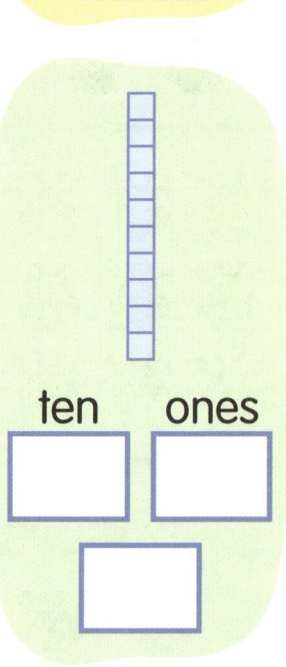

ten   ones

Skill Sharpeners: Math • EMC 8251 • © Evan-Moor Corp.

Find the Tens

Skill: Count by 10s

Count by **tens** to **100**. Then write the numbers.

| 10 | 20 | | | | | | | | |

Use   gray or  brown to color the shapes that have the numbers above.

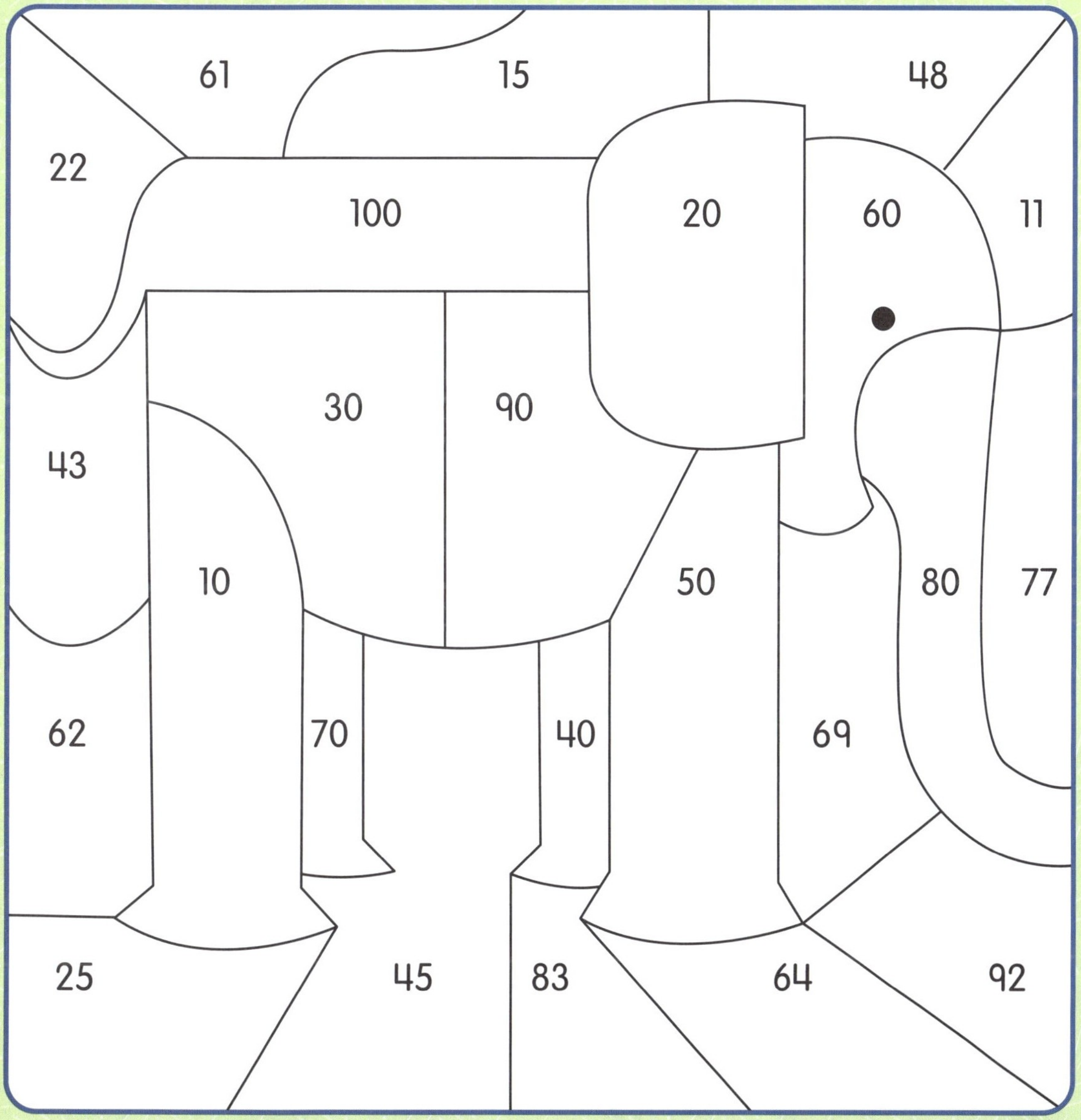

On Safari

Animal Toys

Draw lines to match.

 1¢ penny

 5¢ nickel

 8¢

 12¢

 10¢

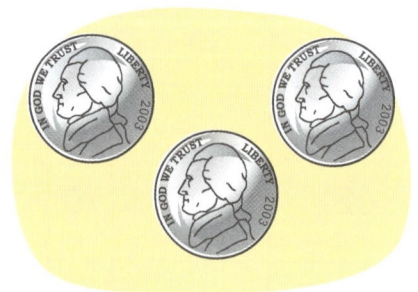

 15¢

Skill: Determine the value of coins

Fact Families

Fact families are addition facts and subtraction facts that have the same 3 numbers. Make fact families.

3 numbers: 7, 5, 12

2 addition facts
7 + 5 = 12
5 + 7 = 12

2 subtraction facts
12 − 5 = 7
12 − 7 = 5

Skills: Add and subtract within 20; Use addition and subtraction strategies (addition-subtraction relationship)

8, 3, 11

___ + ___ = ___
___ + ___ = ___
___ − ___ = ___
___ − ___ = ___

9, 4, 13

___ − ___ = ___
___ − ___ = ___
___ + ___ = ___
___ + ___ = ___

8, 4, 12

___ + ___ = ___
___ + ___ = ___
___ − ___ = ___
___ − ___ = ___

8, 6, 14

___ − ___ = ___
___ − ___ = ___
___ + ___ = ___
___ + ___ = ___

Let's Go Camping

Lots of Trees

Skill: Use addition strategies (counting on)

Count on to find the sums.

9 + 3 = ?

Start with 9.
Add 3 by counting on.

Solve by counting on. Write the numbers.

8 + 2 = ___

12 + 1 = ___

11 + 3 = ___

9 + 2 = ___

Note: You may need to help your child read the word problems.

Busy Campers

Skills: Solve word problems; Add three numbers

Read. Solve the problems.

3 campers went fishing. 5 campers went swimming. 4 campers went hiking. How many campers were there?

_____ campers

Raul is collecting leaves. He finds 4 red leaves, 3 orange leaves, and 7 yellow leaves. How many leaves did he find?

_____ leaves

Kim, Candy, and Maria went fishing. Each girl caught 5 fish. How many fish did they catch in all?

_____ fish

Tony saw birds at camp. He saw 7 jays, 3 hawks, and 4 quails. How many birds did he see?

_____ birds

Write a word problem about this picture. Then write a number sentence for it.

_____

_____

_____ + _____ + _____ = _____

Let's Go Camping

Sleepyheads

Skill: Subtract within 20

Use the sleeping bags to help you subtract.

13 − 4 = ___   13 − 6 = ___

13 − 7 = ___   13 − 8 = ___

13 − 9 = ___   13 − 5 = ___

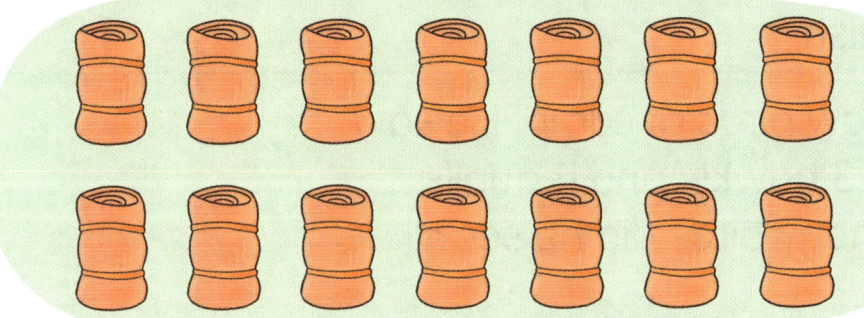

14 − 6 = ___   14 − 4 = ___

14 − 7 = ___   14 − 9 = ___

14 − 8 = ___   14 − 5 = ___

Note: You may need to help your child read the word problems.

A Week at Camp

Skills:
Solve word problems;
Add and subtract within 20

Read. Solve the problems.

There were 13 scouts in Red Troop. 9 scouts went canoeing. The rest of the scouts went fishing. How many scouts went fishing?

_____ scouts went fishing.

Gabe collected 14 leaves. He gave 5 leaves to a friend. How many leaves did Gabe have left?

Gabe had _____ leaves left.

Mary Anne toasted 8 marshmallows. Katie toasted 6 marshmallows. How many marshmallows were toasted in all?

_____ marshmallows were toasted in all.

Blue Troop put up 12 tents. The wind blew down 8 tents. How many tents were still standing?

_____ tents were still standing.

Let's Go Camping

Camping Gear

Read the graph. Then answer the questions.

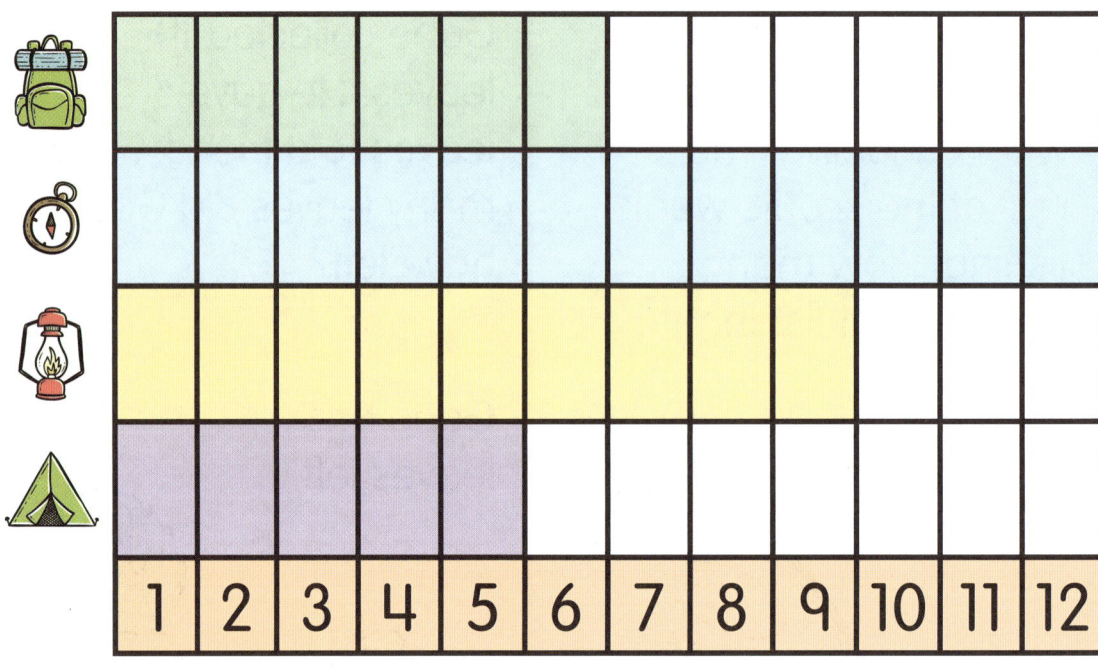

How many 🎒 are there? _____

How many ⛺ are there? _____

Are there more 🧭 or more 🏮?

Write the problems. Then answer them.

How many more 🏮 than 🎒 are there?

How many ⛺ and 🎒 are there in all?

Through the Woods

This is a long path. Count by ones. Write the numbers.

Ten people sleep in each tent. Count by tens to find out how many people are sleeping.

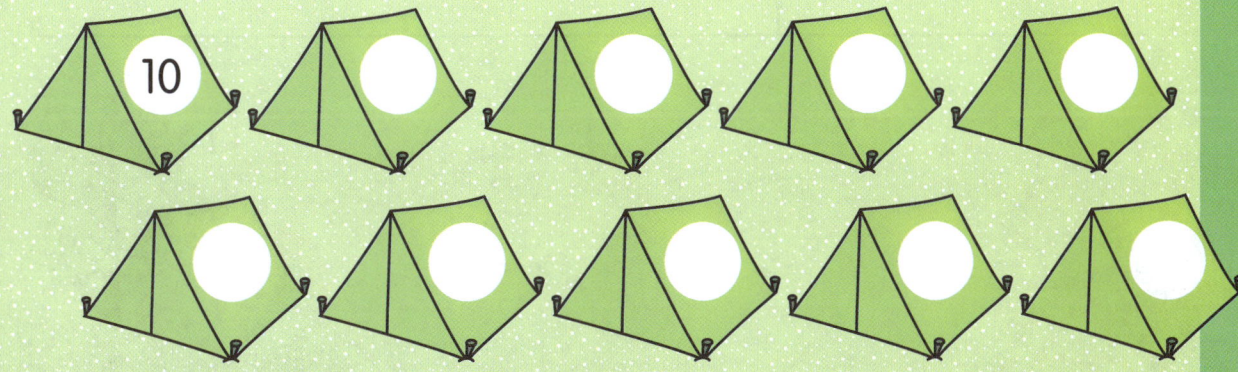

Before, After, or Between

Skill: Count within 100

Write the missing number.

after	before	between
21 ___	___ 47	29 ___ 31
39 ___	___ 50	43 ___ 45
45 ___	___ 36	38 ___ 40
50 ___	___ 64	51 ___ 53
64 ___	___ 21	67 ___ 69
77 ___	___ 92	80 ___ 82
99 ___	___ 63	87 ___ 89

How Many Sticks?

How many tens and ones do you see?

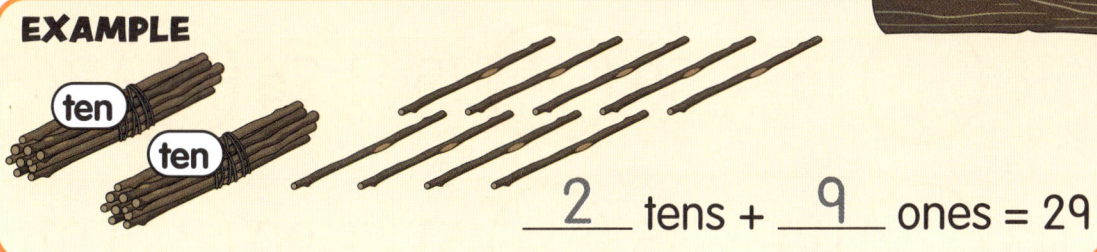

EXAMPLE

__2__ tens + __9__ ones = 29

____ tens + ____ ones = 26

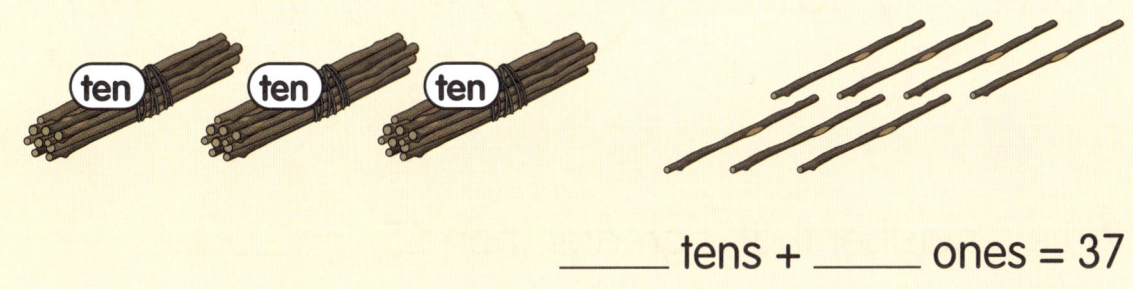

____ tens + ____ ones = 37

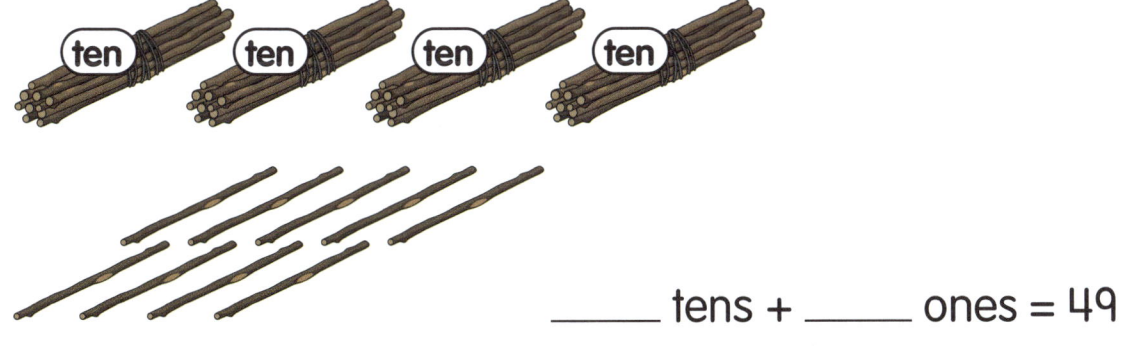

____ tens + ____ ones = 49

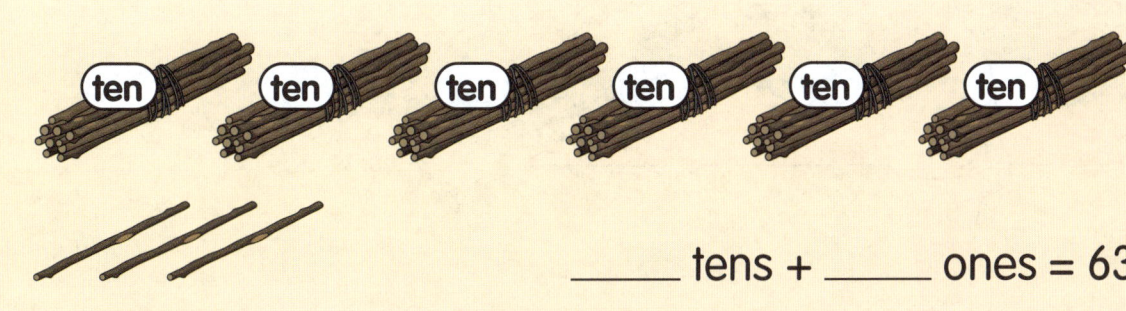

____ tens + ____ ones = 63

Comparing Fun

Skill:
Compare two-digit numbers

Write >, <, or =.

18 ◯ 16	14 ◯ 19	26 ◯ 26
43 ◯ 40	15 ◯ 51	90 ◯ 91
37 ◯ 73	21 ◯ 12	48 ◯ 44
89 ◯ 98	71 ◯ 74	77 ◯ 77

Write a number that is greater than 25. ______

Write a number that is less than 52. ______

Write a number that is equal to 99. ______

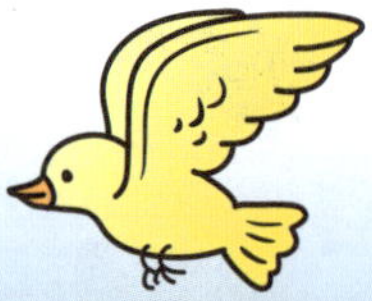

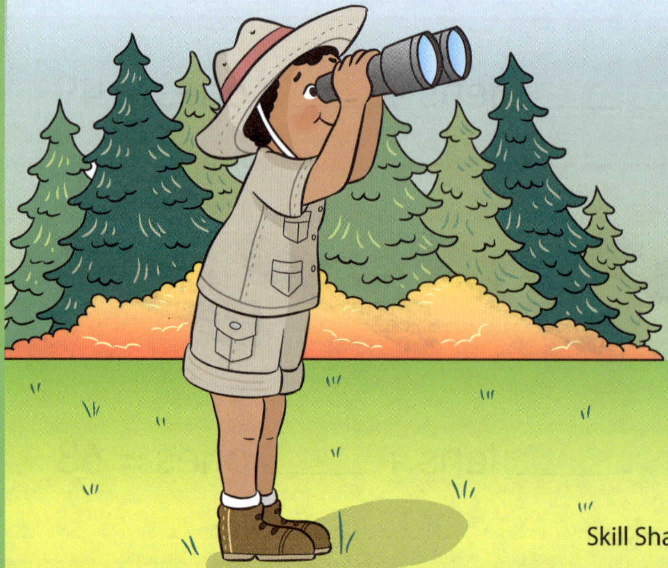

More or Less

Skills: Count within 100; Find 10 more and less than a number

1	2	3	4	5	6	7	8	9	10
11	12	13	14	15	16	17	18	19	20
21	22	23	24	25	26	27	28	29	30
31	32	33	34	35	36	37	38	39	40
41	42	43	44	45	46	47	48	49	50
51	52	53	54	55	56	57	58	59	60
61	62	63	64	65	66	67	68	69	70
71	72	73	74	75	76	77	78	79	80
81	82	83	84	85	86	87	88	89	90
91	92	93	94	95	96	97	98	99	100

Write the missing numbers.
Use the number chart to help you.

	1 more	1 less	10 more	10 less
12	___	___	___	___
25	___	___	___	___
34	___	___	___	___
49	___	___	___	___
87	___	___	___	___

Let's Go Camping

TEST YOUR SKILLS

Add or subtract.

5 + 8 = ____   7 + 7 = ____   5 + 9 = ____

13 – 4 = ____   13 – 5 = ____   15 – 7 = ____

Write the number that comes before, after, or between.

____, 65   36, ____   79, ____, 81

Write a number sentence to solve the problem.

8 campers went hiking. Then 6 campers joined them. How many campers went hiking?

____ + ____ = ____

Count by 1s.

75 ___ ___ ___ ___ ___ ___ ___ 83

How many tens and ones? How many in all?

____ tens + ____ ones = ____

Let's Go Camping

A Tasty Crop

Add or subtract. Then find the apples with answers that are the same as **3 + 3 + 3**. Color those apples red. Color the other apples yellow.

7 + 8

15 − 7

15 − 8

8 + 8

16 − 8

16 − 7

8 + 7

16 − 9

15 − 6

9 + 7

6 + 9

15 − 9

Skill: Add and subtract within 20

Fruity Fun

Fruity Facts

Add or subtract.

6 + 7 = ___
7 + 6 = ___
13 − 7 = ___
13 − 6 = ___

9 + 5 = ___
5 + 9 = ___
14 − 9 = ___
14 − 5 = ___

8 + 6 = ___
6 + 8 = ___
14 − 6 = ___
14 − 8 = ___

8 + 7 = ___
7 + 8 = ___
15 − 7 = ___
15 − 8 = ___

9 + 6 = ___
6 + 9 = ___
15 − 6 = ___
15 − 9 = ___

9 + 7 = ___
7 + 9 = ___
16 − 7 = ___
16 − 9 = ___

Skill: Add and subtract within 20

What's Growing?

Note: You may need to help your child read the word problems.

Read. Write the problems. Solve them.

Dana planted 16 seeds. 7 seeds sprouted. How many seeds did not sprout?

_____ seeds did not sprout.

Jamal picked 8 pears from a tree. Leah picked 7 pears from another tree. How many pears did they pick in all?

They picked _____ pears.

A tree had 8 big plums and 8 little plums. How many plums were on the tree?

There were _____ plums on the tree.

Kimi's tree had 15 apples. Ahmed's tree had 9 apples. How many more apples did Kimi's tree have than Ahmed's tree?

Kimi's tree had _____ more apples.

Skills: Solve word problems; Add and subtract within 20

Fruity Fun

Bunches of Grapes

Skill: Compose numbers with tens and ones

Each bunch has 10 grapes.
Add the grapes that are in each set.

This is 1 ten.

__3__ tens + __5__ ones = __35__

__30__ + __5__ = __35__

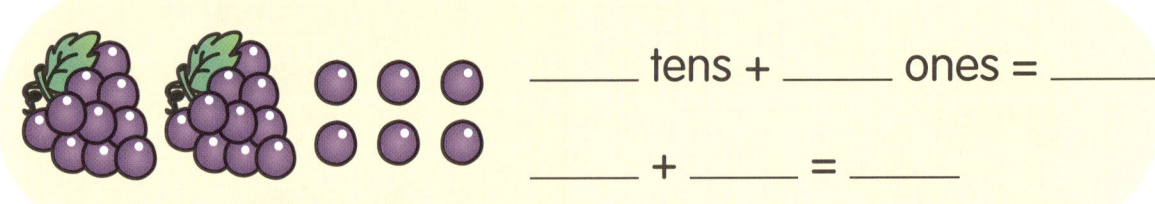

____ tens + ____ ones = ____

____ + ____ = ____

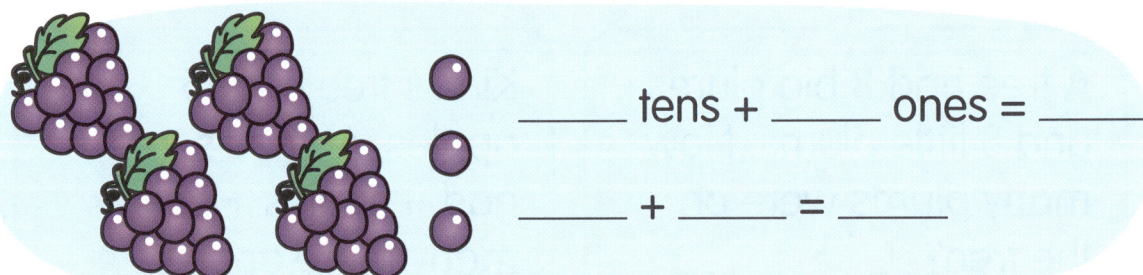

____ tens + ____ ones = ____

____ + ____ = ____

Add.

60 + 7 = ____   90 + 2 = ____

70 + 8 = ____   50 + 5 = ____

Add the Apples

Each basket has 10 apples. Add the apples in each set.

 This is 1 ten.

Skill: Compose numbers with tens

__2__ tens + __3__ tens = __5__ tens

__20__ + __30__ = __50__

____ tens + ____ tens = ____ tens

____ + ____ = ____

____ tens + ____ tens = ____ tens

____ + ____ = ____

Add.

50 + 20 = ____   70 + 10 = ____

30 + 60 = ____   10 + 40 = ____

Find the Fruits

Skill: Add multiples of 10

Add. Then use the code to color.

- red = 60
- green = 70
- orange = 80
- yellow = 90

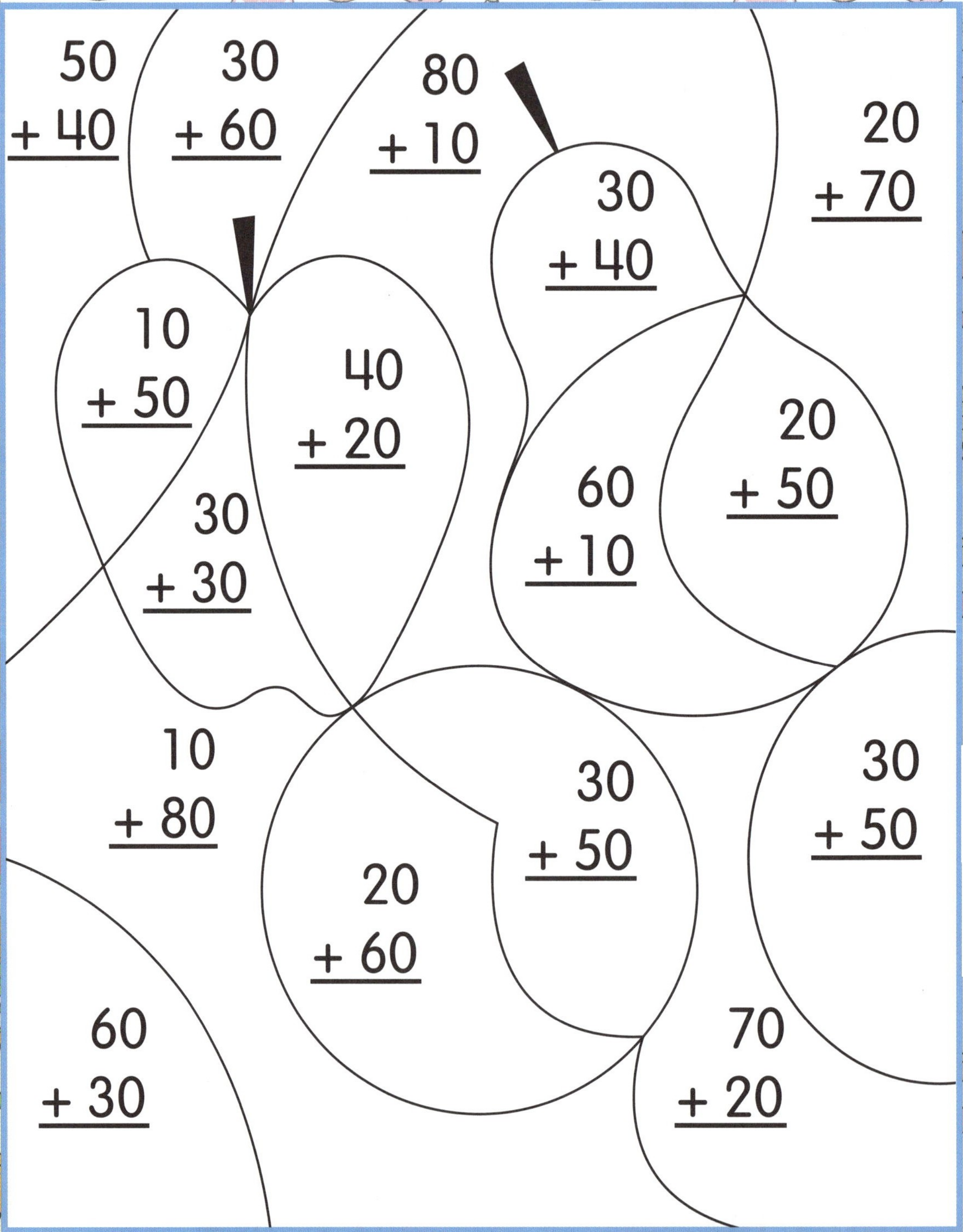

50 + 40	30 + 60
80 + 10	20 + 70
30 + 40	10 + 50
40 + 20	20 + 50
30 + 30	60 + 10
10 + 80	30 + 50
20 + 60	30 + 50
60 + 30	70 + 20

Fruity Fun

A Fruity Path

Count by 5s to get to the fruit trees.
Fill in the missing numbers.

5, 50, 95

Skill: Count by 5s

Fruity Fun

Add or subtract.

7 + 8 = ____   16 − 8 = ____   15 − 6 = ____

9 + 7 = ____   15 − 7 = ____   16 − 9 = ____

Count by 5s.

____ ____ ____ ____ ____ ____ ____ ____ ____ ____

____ ____ ____ ____ ____ ____ ____ ____ ____ ____

Add.

____ tens + ____ tens = ____ tens

____ + ____ = ____

20 + 8 = ____   70 + 5 = ____

60 + 9 = ____   30 + 40 = ____

10 + 50 = ____   50 + 40 = ____

Icy Homes

Skill: Add within 20

Add. Color the igloos with a sum of 17 yellow.
Color the igloos with a sum of 18 purple.

8 + 7 = ___

8 + 9 = ___

9 + 6 = ___

8 + 8 = ___

9 + 7 = ___

9 + 8 = ___

9 + 9 = ___

8 + 6 = ___

Walrus Numbers

Skills:
Use addition and subtraction strategies (addition-subtraction relationship); Add and subtract within 20

Use each set of numbers to make two addition problems and two subtraction problems.

Polar Animals

Note: You may need to help your child read the word problems.

Skills: Solve word problems; Add and subtract within 20

Read. Write the problems. Solve them.

9 penguins were swimming in the sea. 8 more penguins jumped in. How many penguins were swimming in the sea then?

☐ + ☐ = ☐

There were ____ penguins swimming in the sea then.

16 walruses were lying on the ice. 9 walruses slid back into the sea. How many walruses were still on the ice?

☐ − ☐ = ☐

There were ____ walruses still on the ice.

Polar Bear saw 6 seals in the morning and 9 seals in the afternoon. How many seals did Polar Bear see that day?

☐ + ☐ = ☐

Polar Bear saw ____ seals that day.

18 seals were playing in the water. 9 seals swam away. How many seals were still playing?

☐ − ☐ = ☐

There were ____ seals still playing.

Chilly Capers

Seeing Double

Skill: Use addition and subtraction strategies (doubles)

Add.

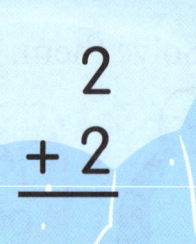
2
+ 2

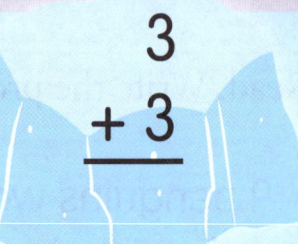
3
+ 3

1
+ 1

5
+ 5

4
+ 4

6
+ 6

8
+ 8

7
+ 7

9
+ 9

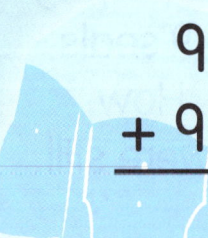

10
+ 10

Use the doubles addition facts to help you subtract.

```
  12        16        18        14
 − 6       − 8       − 9       − 7
```

Catch of the Day

Skills: Add two-digit numbers; Add multiples of 10

Add.

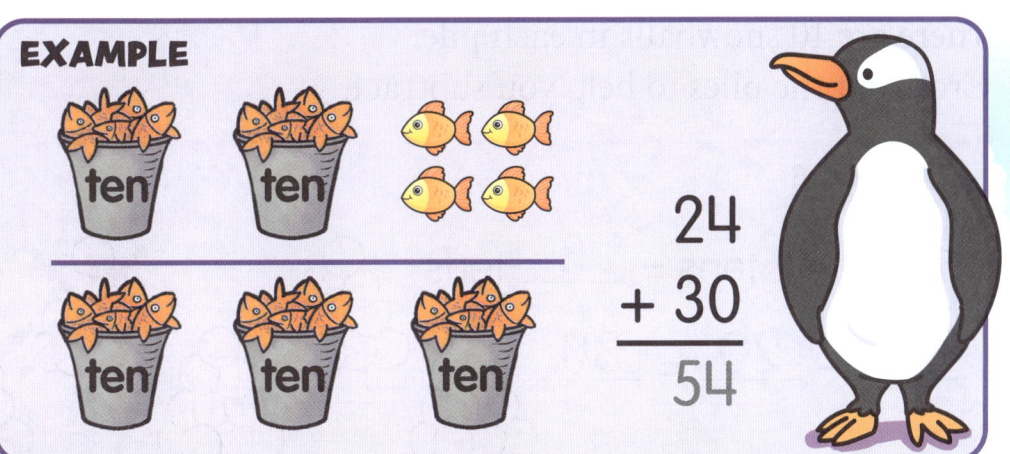

- 15 + 10
- 24 + 20
- 18 + 60
- 27 + 20
- 39 + 30
- 27 + 40
- 21 + 50
- 16 + 70
- 83 + 10
- 52 + 30
- 35 + 40

Chilly Capers

Snowball Subtraction

Skill: Subtract multiples of 10

There are 10 snowballs in each pile.
Cross out the piles to help you subtract.

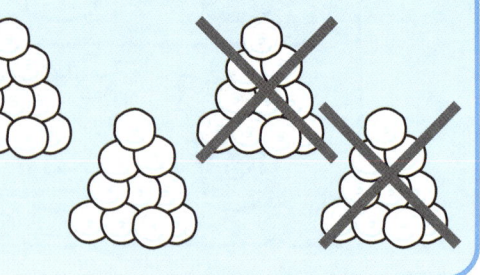

EXAMPLE

5 tens − 2 tens = __3__ tens

__50__ − __20__ = __30__

3 tens − 1 ten = ____ tens

____ − ____ = ____

4 tens − 3 tens = ____ ten

____ − ____ = ____

5 tens − 3 tens = ____ tens

____ − ____ = ____

Subtract.

```
  60        80        70        90
− 50      − 30      − 10      − 40
----      ----      ----      ----
```

Let It Snow!

Add or subtract.

15 + 30 =

20 + 60 =

82 − 20 =

60 + 30 =

90 − 20 =

70 − 50 =

40 + 40 =

60 − 30 =

30 + 40 =

Winter Stickers

Skill: Determine value of coins

Add the coins. Write the price on the tag.

 penny 1¢    nickel 5¢    dime 10¢

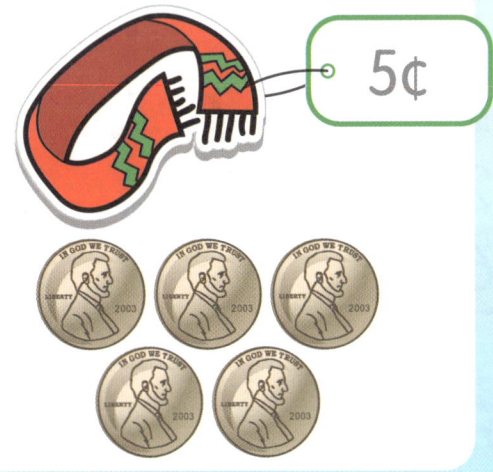 5¢

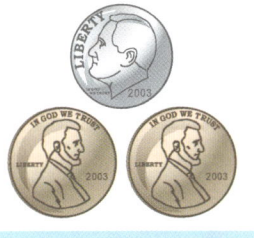

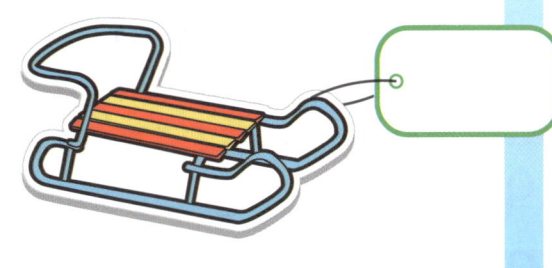

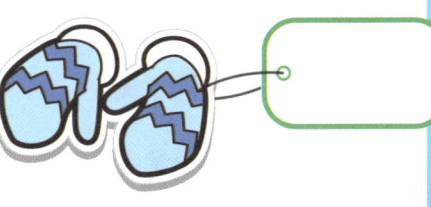

Fun in the Snow

Skill: Count by 2s

Count the mittens by 2s.

2   4   ___   ___   ___

12   ___   ___   ___   ___

Count by 2s to slide down the hill.

Connect the dots. Color.

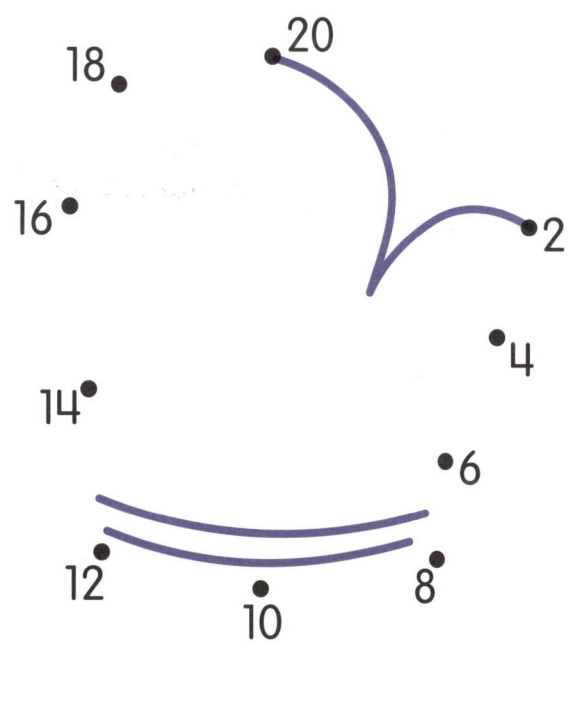

Fish-Eating Contest

Skill: Read a graph

Use the graph to find out how many fish the animals ate. Then answer the questions.

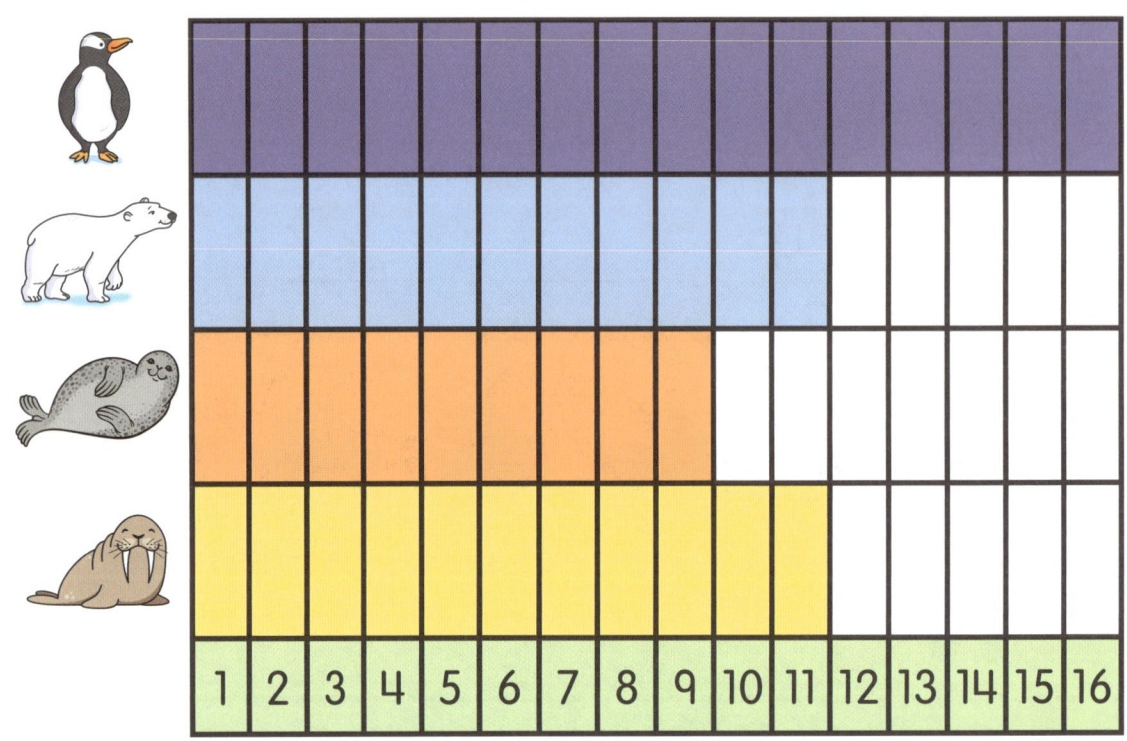

How many fish did each animal eat?

 _____  _____  _____  _____

Which animal ate the most fish?

Which animal ate the fewest fish?

Polar Bear and Seal ate _____ fish in all.

Penguin ate _____ more fish than Walrus.

Add or subtract.

8 + 9 = ___   9 + 9 = ___   9 + 8 = ___

17 − 9 = ___   17 − 8 = ___   18 − 9 = ___

Count by 2s.

___, ___, 6, ___, 10, 12, 14, ___, ___, 20

There were 9 gray seals and 8 brown seals.
How many seals were there?

___ + ___ = ___   There were ___ seals.

Add or subtract.

```
  49        27        80        70
+ 50      + 30      − 60      − 20
----      ----      ----      ----
```

Write the time.

___ : ___   ___ : ___

Colorful Balloons

Skill: Use addition strategies (make 10)

First add two numbers to make 10. Then add the last number.

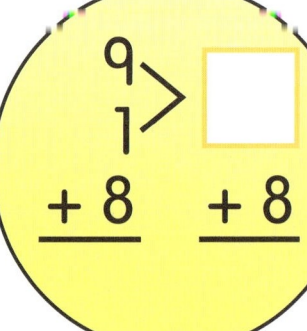
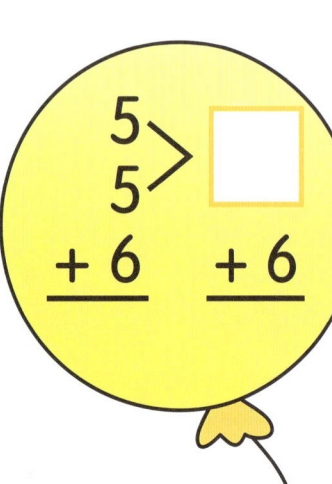

Balls in the Air

Circle the balls needed to make a group of 10.
Then finish adding the rest.

7 + 5 = ?

7 + _3_ = 10   10 + _2_ = _12_

9 + 4 = ?

9 + ___ = 10   10 + ___ = ___

6 + 7 = ?

6 + ___ = 10   10 + ___ = ___

8 + 6 = ?

8 + ___ = 10   10 + ___ = ___

Skill: Use addition strategies (make 10)

At the Fair

Number Carts

Skill: Add within 20

Add.

6 + ___ = 13
8 + ___ = 14

___ + 9 = 18
___ + 7 = 12

9 + ___ = 17
5 + ___ = 14

___ + 8 = 16
___ + 9 = 15

Fill your own cart.

___ + ___ = ___
___ + ___ = ___

A Roller Coaster Ride

Add.

```
  46      20      70      51      73
+ 30    + 30    +  8    + 40    + 20
```

```
  36      50      80      42      15
+ 60    + 30    +  9    + 40    + 40
```

```
  17      12      29      10      20
+ 60    + 80    + 20    + 50    + 50
```

Skills: Add two-digit numbers; Add multiples of 10

Tasty Treats

Note: You may need to help your child read the word problems.

Read. Write the problems. Solve them.

Kai sold ice cream cones at the fair. He sold 35 cones before lunch. He sold 40 cones after lunch. How many ice cream cones did he sell at the fair?

Kai sold _____ ice cream cones.

Jason bought a bag of peanuts. There were 50 peanuts in the bag. Jason ate 20 peanuts. How many peanuts were left?

There were _____ peanuts left.

Anna sold 27 bags of popcorn. Sam sold 30 bags of popcorn. How many bags did they sell together?

They sold _____ bags of popcorn.

---

80 people bought cotton candy yesterday. 60 people bought cotton candy today. How many more people bought cotton candy yesterday than today?

_____ more people bought cotton candy yesterday.

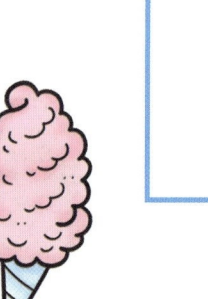 

Down We Go!

Skills:
Subtract two-digit numbers; Subtract multiples of 10

Cross out tens to help you subtract.

 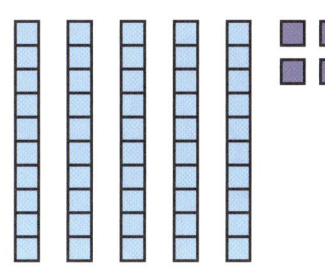

54 – 20 = ___

38 – 20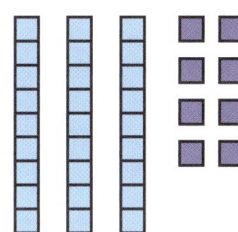

38 – 20 = ___

42 – 10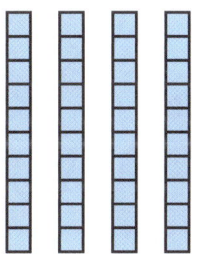

42 – 10 = ___

57 – 40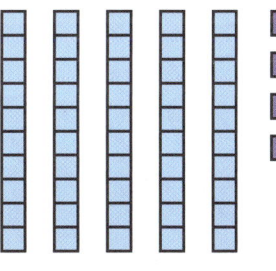

57 – 40 = ___

69 – 30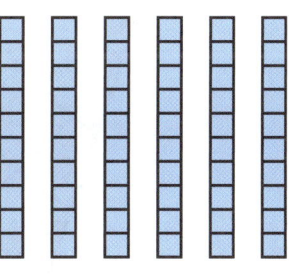

69 – 30 = ___

At the Fair

Cool Subtraction

Subtract.

65 − 40 =

81 − 50 =

39 − 10 =

75 − 30 =

28 − 10 =

47 − 20 =

96 − 70 =

52 − 40 =

88 − 60 =

73 − 20 =

Equal Parts

Skill: Identify equal shares

How many equal parts are there?

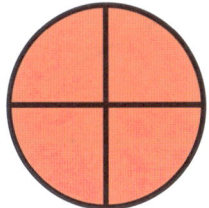  

____ parts   ____ parts   ____ part

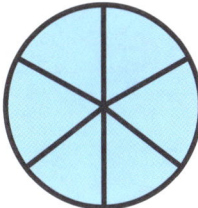 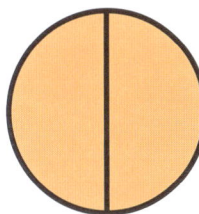 

____ parts   ____ parts   ____ parts

Which shapes have 2 **equal** parts? Circle them.

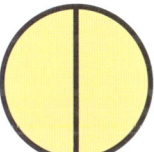 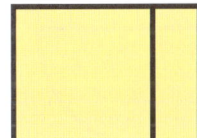  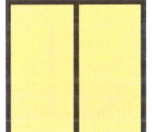 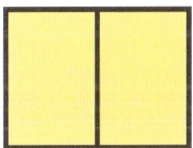

Which shapes have 4 **equal** parts? Circle them.

 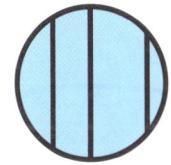 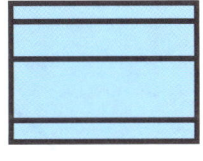  

At the Fair

Fraction Fun

Skill: Identify equal shares

Color one half of each shape green.

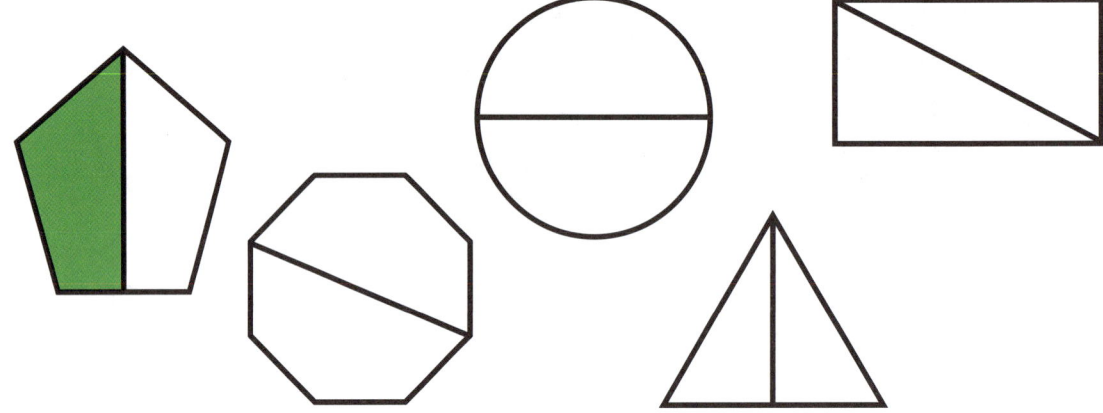

Color one fourth of each shape blue.

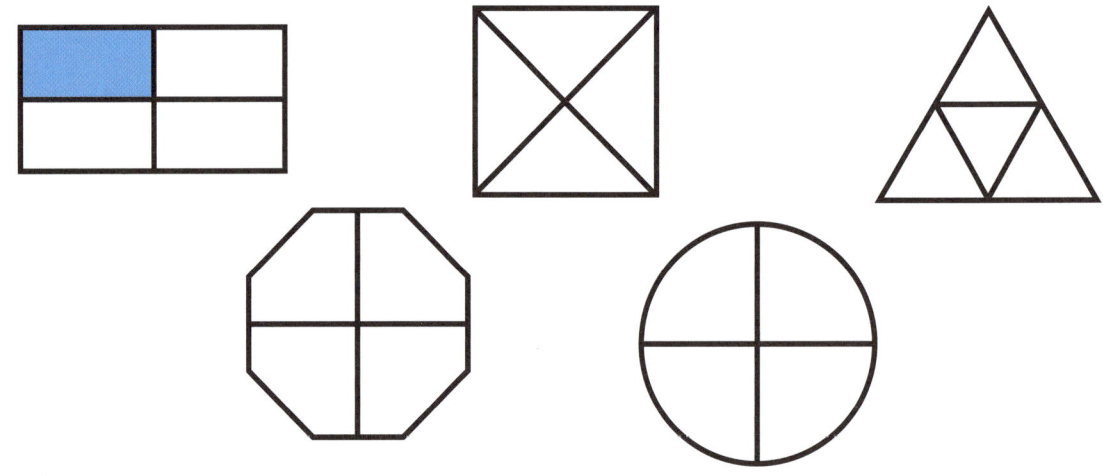

Draw a line to make 2 equal parts. Color one half green.

Draw lines to make 4 equal parts. Color one fourth blue.

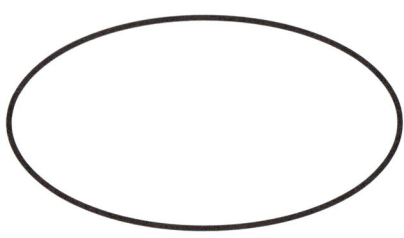

When Will They Go?

Six families are going to the fair at different times. Draw lines to match the clocks.

Jones family

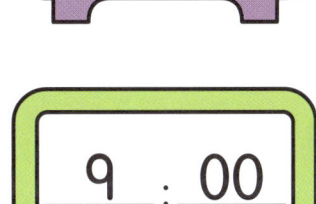
2 : 00

9 : 00

Eng family

Lee family

11 : 30

8 : 30

Santos family

Sidhu family

10 : 30

Miller family

12 : 00

Skill: Tell time to the half hour

The Great Caterpillar Race

The fair had a Great Caterpillar Race. How long were the racers?

_____ centimeters

_____ centimeters

_____ centimeters

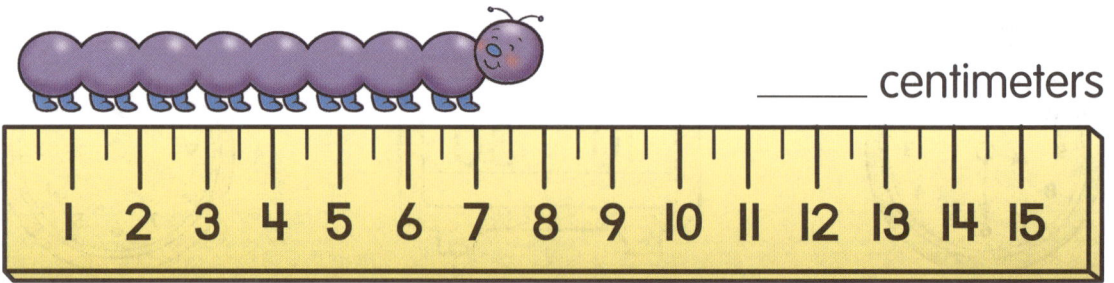

_____ centimeters

Which caterpillar was the longest—orange, green, blue, or purple? _____

Skill: Measure length using centimeters

Fill in the missing numbers.

7 + ____ = 13   8 + ____ = 15   6 + ____ = 15

____ + 9 = 17   ____ + 5 = 14   ____ + 8 = 16

Add or subtract.

78 – 30 = ____   63 + 20 = ____

45 + 20 = ____   91 – 50 = ____

Blair sold 56 bags of popcorn on Monday and 40 bags on Tuesday. How many bags of popcorn did Blair sell?

Blair sold ____ bags of popcorn.

Circle the shapes that have one fourth colored.

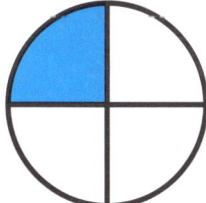 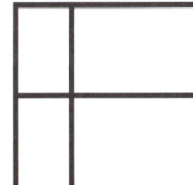  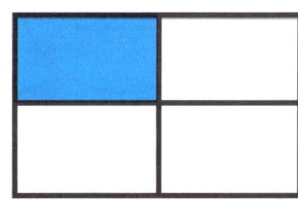

How long?

____ centimeters

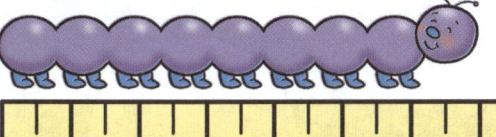

Tennis, Anyone?

Skill: Add three numbers

Use the numbers on the tennis balls to complete each problem.

 3    2    6    0

 12   10   9   5

```
   4          2          8          6
  □          3         1         0
+ 3        + 4        +□        +□
────      ────       ────       ────
  10         □         11         11
```

```
   1         □          2          4
   9         5         □         4
+ 0        + 5        + 4        + 4
────      ────       ────       ────
   □         10         12         □
```

Let's Bowl

Skill: Sequence two-digit numbers

Write the numbers in order from the least to the greatest.

EXAMPLE

15 5 50 → 5   15   50

43 14 34 → ___   ___   ___

76 67 77 → ___   ___   ___

19 99 90 → ___   ___   ___

80 85 58 → ___   ___   ___

Hockey Practice

Skill: Add two-digit numbers

Add. You can break up numbers to help you.

EXAMPLE

31
+ 64 →   30 + 1
          60 + 4
          ―――――――
          90 + 5 = 95

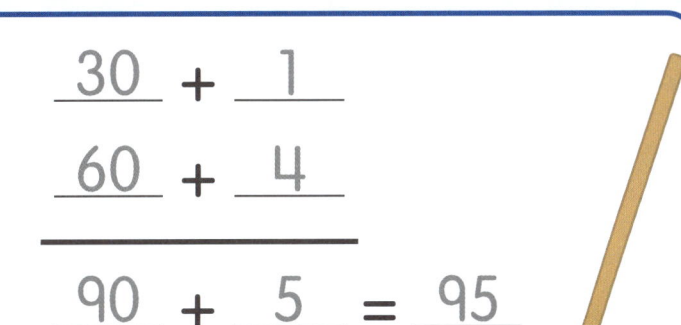

15
+ 42 →   __ + __
          __ + __
          ―――――――
          __ + __ = __

23
+ 75 →   __ + __
          __ + __
          ―――――――
          __ + __ = __

52
+ 24 →   __ + __
          __ + __
          ―――――――
          __ + __ = __

A Great Shot

Skill: Add and subtract two-digit numbers

Add or subtract the **ones** first.
Then add or subtract the **tens**.

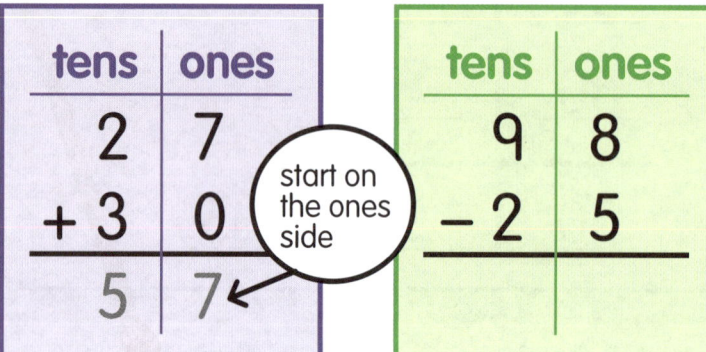

tens	ones
2	7
+3	0
5	7

start on the ones side

tens	ones
9	8
−2	5

tens	ones
1	3
+3	1

tens	ones
6	4
−3	0

tens	ones
6	0
+2	5

tens	ones
3	7
−2	7

tens	ones
8	6
−7	5

tens	ones
7	1
−5	1

tens	ones
5	1
+4	4

You Can Do It!

Skills: Use addition strategies (regrouping); Add two-digit numbers

Sometimes you get an extra ten when you add ones.
Circle the extra ten. Write it. Then add the tens and ones.

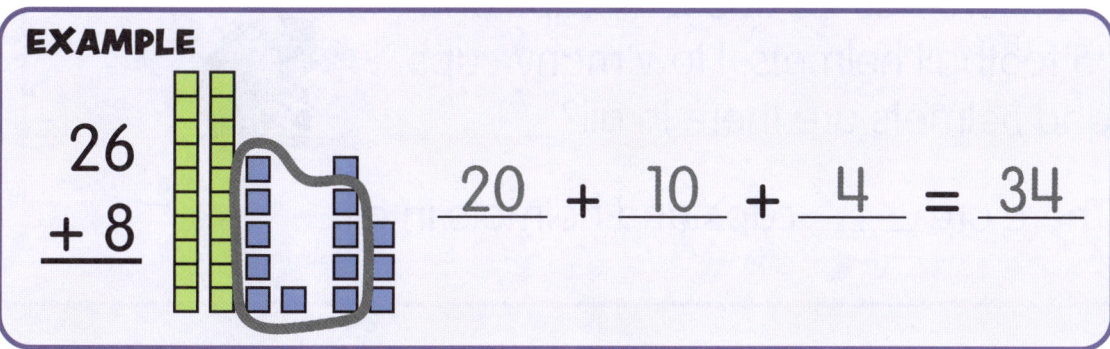

EXAMPLE

26
+ 8

___20___ + ___10___ + ___4___ = ___34___

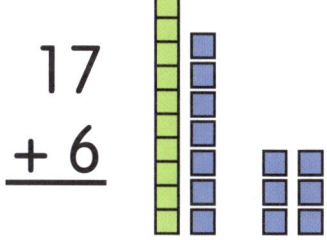

17
+ 6

____ + ____ + ____ = ____

45
+ 9

____ + ____ + ____ = ____

29
+ 7

____ + ____ + ____ = ____

Time for Sports

All Kinds of Sports

Note: You may need to help your child read the word problems.

Skills:
Solve word problems;
Use addition strategies (regrouping);
Add two-digit numbers

Read. Write the problems. Solve them.

The store has 23 baseball caps and 15 football helmets. How many caps and helmets are there in all?

There are _____ caps and helmets in all.

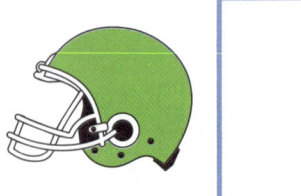

Lily made 15 baskets. Joy made 9 baskets. How many baskets did Lily and Joy make for the team?

Lily and Joy made _____ baskets for the team.

Quinn shot 19 arrows at a round target. Then he shot 8 arrows at a square target. How many arrows did he shoot in all?

Quinn shot _____ arrows in all.

Damian ran 14 laps this morning and 12 laps this afternoon. How many laps did Damian run today?

Damian ran _____ laps today.

Off to the Game

Help the family get to the sports stadium. Count by 5s to 100. Write the numbers on the road.

Skill: Count by 5s

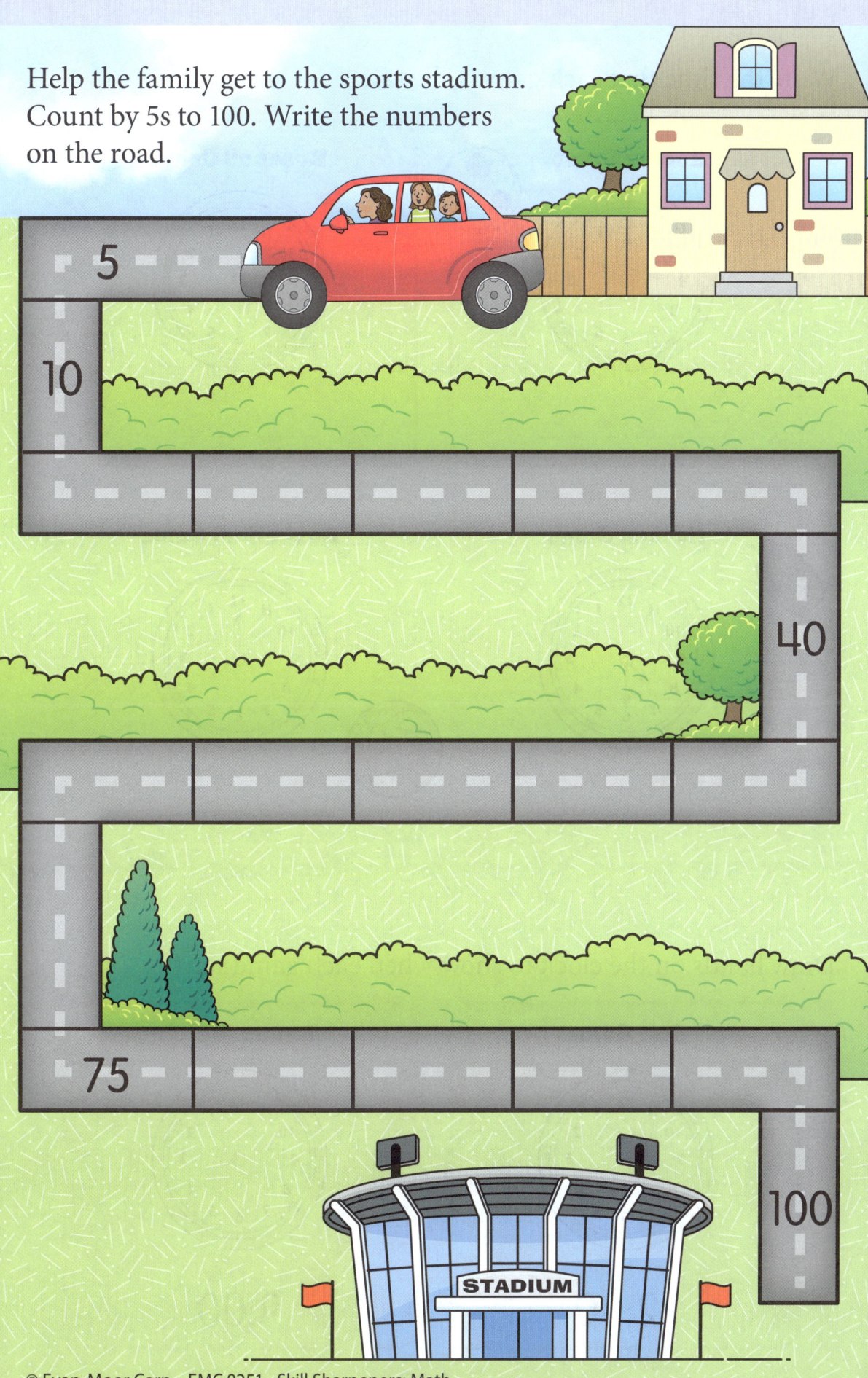

Let the Games Begin!

Skill:
Tell time to the half hour

Time for Sports

Write the time that each game will start.

Soccer Game

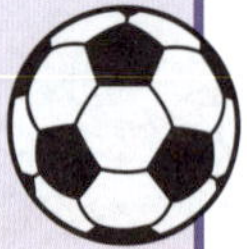
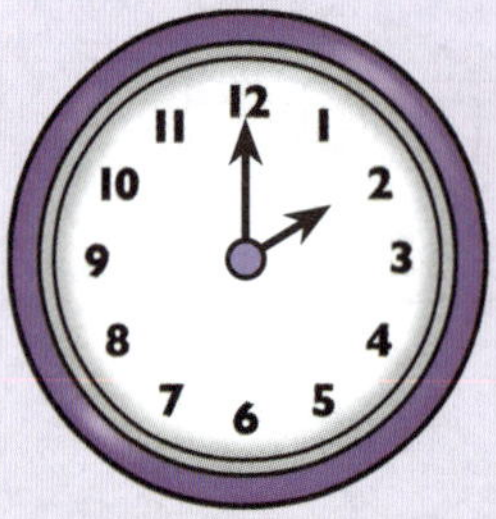

_____ : _____

Baseball Game

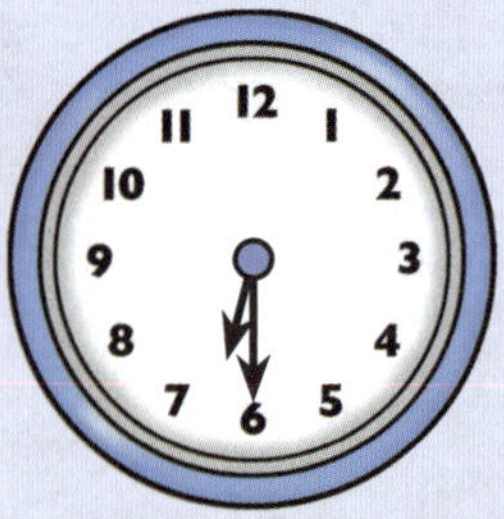
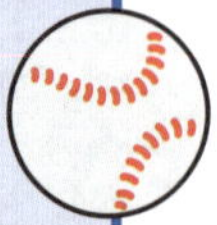

_____ : _____

Hockey Game

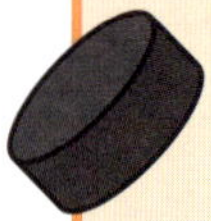
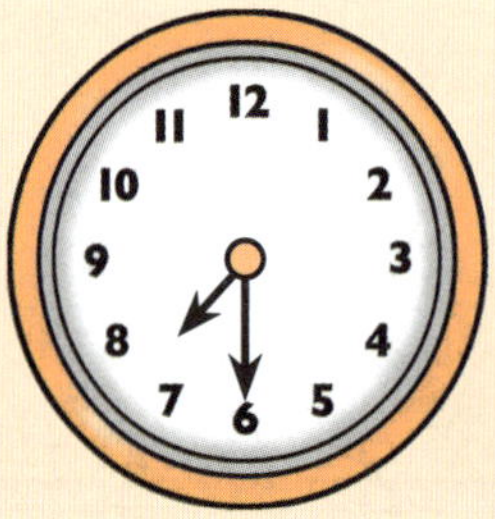

_____ : _____

Basketball Game

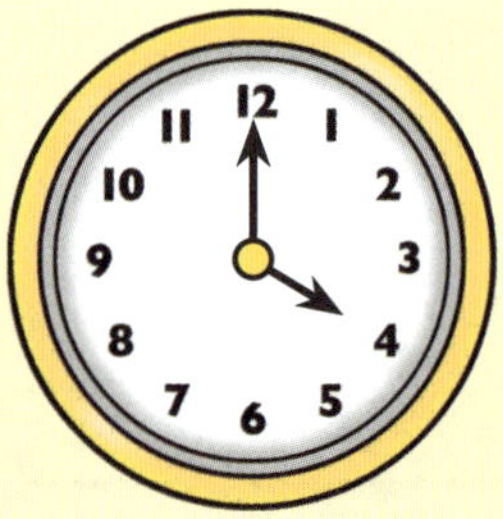
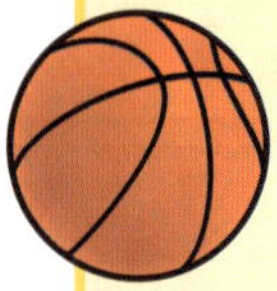

_____ : _____

Draw hands on the clock to show when each game starts.

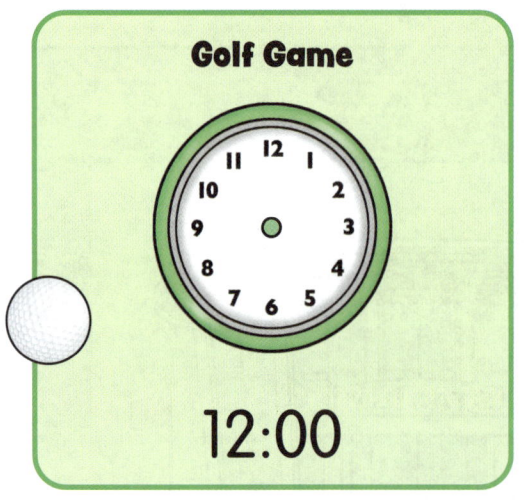

Golf Game

12:00

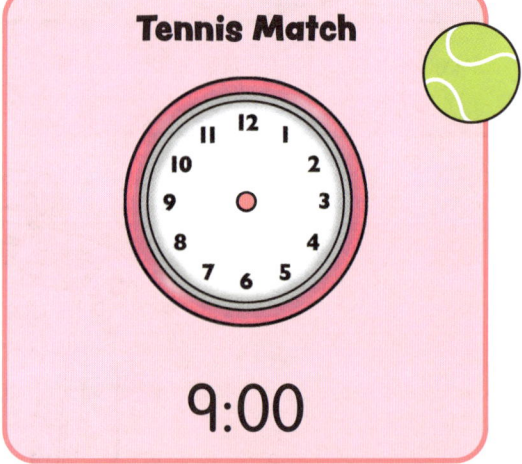

Tennis Match

9:00

Basketball Schedule

Dylan, Kelly, Mia, and Lin will play basketball today. The table shows when their teams will practice.

Practice Schedule	
Dylan's Team	1:00
Kelly's Team	1:30
Mia's Team	2:30
Lin's Team	4:00

Use the table to answer the questions.

Who will play basketball first? _____

Who will practice at 2:30? _____

What time is the last practice? _____

Who will practice after Mia? _____

What time will Kelly practice? _____

Will Mia start before or after 3:00? _____

Skill: Read a data table

At the Sports Store

Skill: Read a graph

Use the graph to answer the questions.

| | 1 | 2 | 3 | 4 | 5 | 6 | 7 | 8 | 9 | 10 |

How many?

Write a question about the graph.

_____

_____

Write the answer to your question.

_____

_____

Which Sport Do You Like Best?

Mr. Tran's class picked the sport they liked best. Look at the chart. Count the tally marks.

Skill: Read a tally

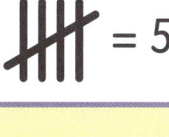 = 5

football	𝍫𝍫𝍫
baseball	𝍫𝍫	
soccer	𝍫𝍫𝍫𝍫 ||
basketball	𝍫 |||

Answer the questions.

Which sports are listed on the chart?
_____

Which sport was picked the most? _____

Which sport was picked the least? _____

How many children picked football? _____

Make a red tally mark by the sport you like best.

Time for Sports

Add.

```
   5        26        □         55
  □        + 5       + 2       + 34
  + 2       ──       ──        ──
  ──        □         11        □
   8
```

Count by 5s.

35, ____, ____, ____   70, ____, ____, ____

Use the tally about playing sports to answer the questions.

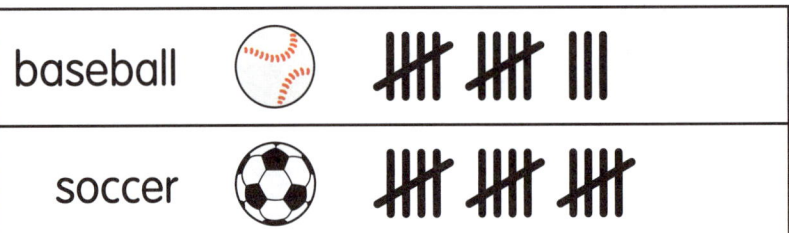

𝍷𝍷𝍷𝍷𝍶 = 5

How many children play baseball? ____

How many children play soccer? ____

Read. Answer the questions.

Keisha made 14 baskets. Devon made 9 baskets.

How many baskets did they make in all? ____ baskets

How many more baskets did Keisha make than Devon?

____ more

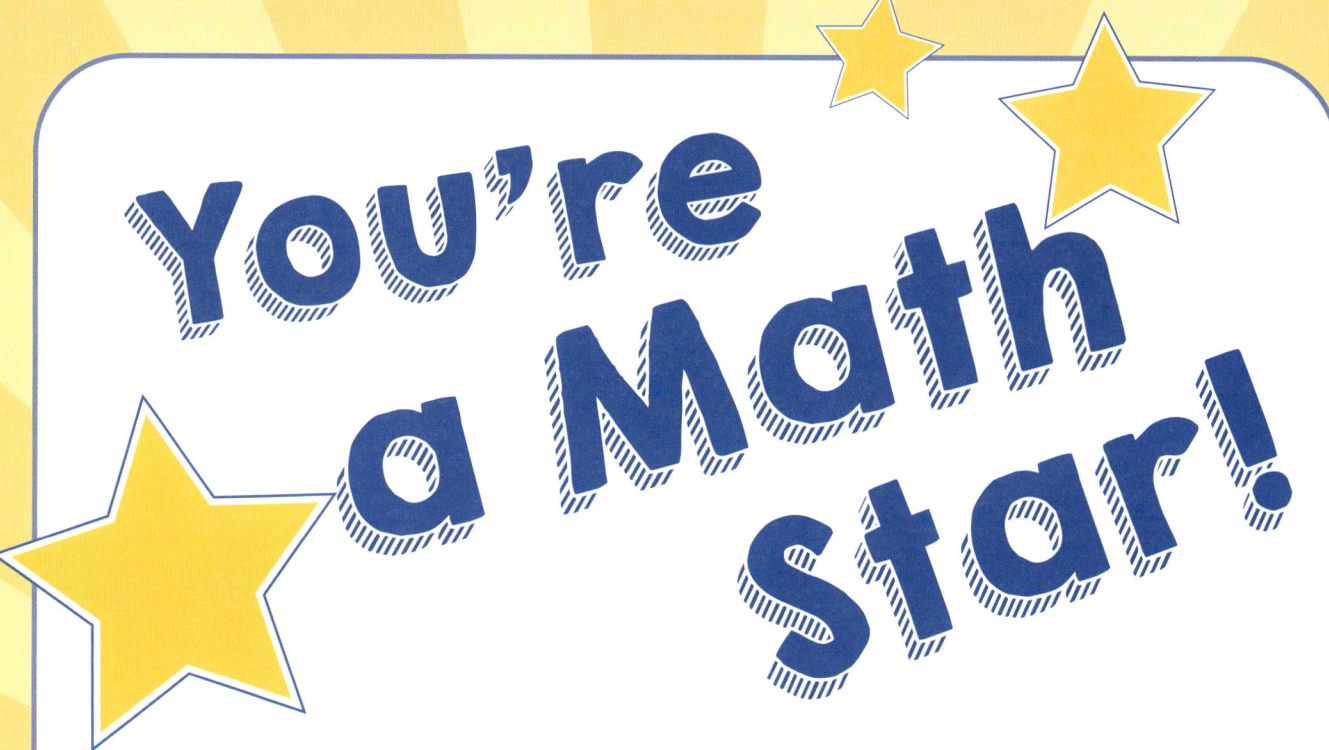

_____
Name

completed
Skill Sharpeners: Math

Answer Key

Page 6
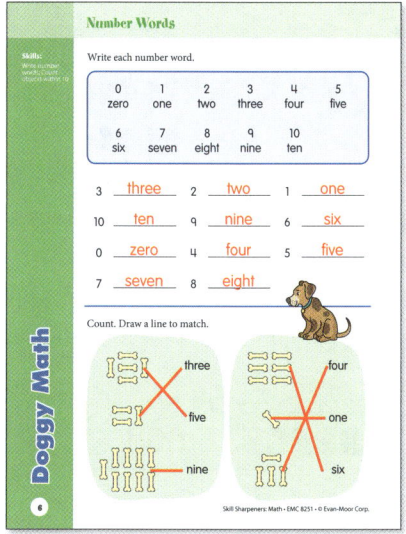

Page 7
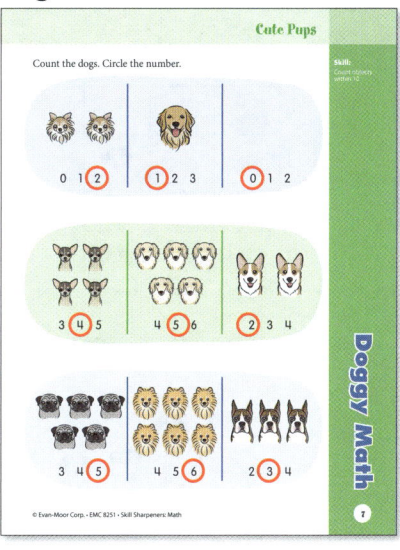

Page 8

Page 9
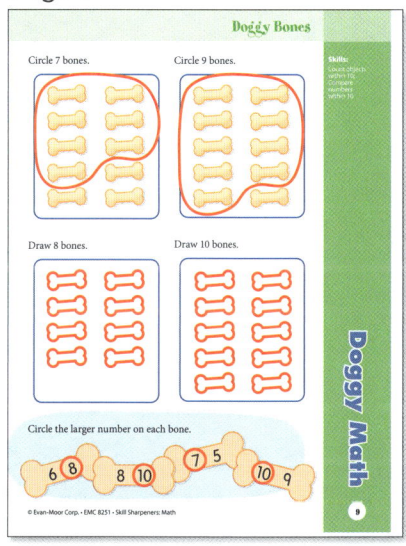

Page 10
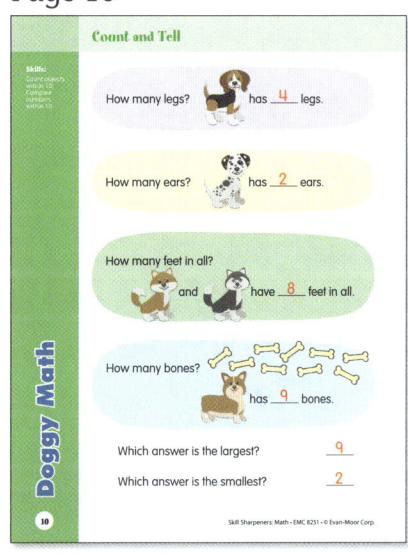

Page 11
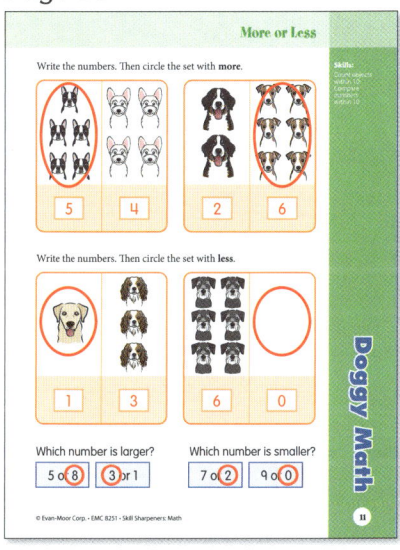

Page 12
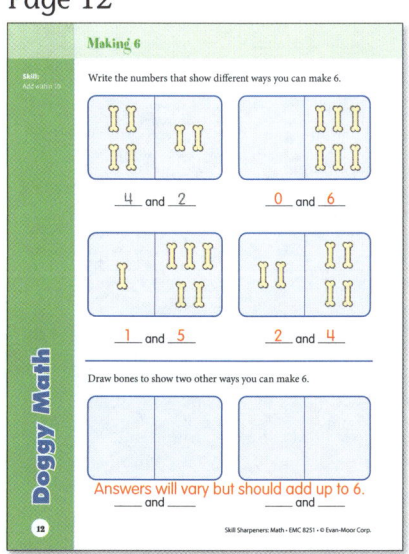

Page 13
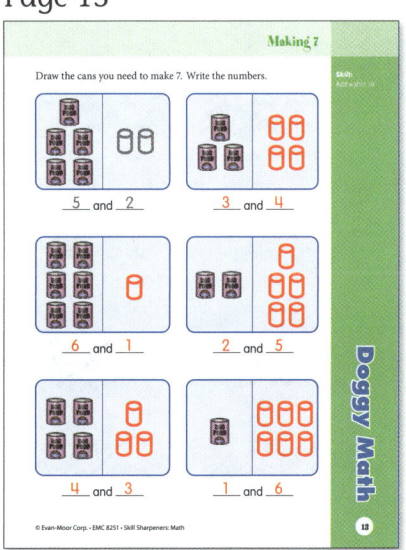

Page 14
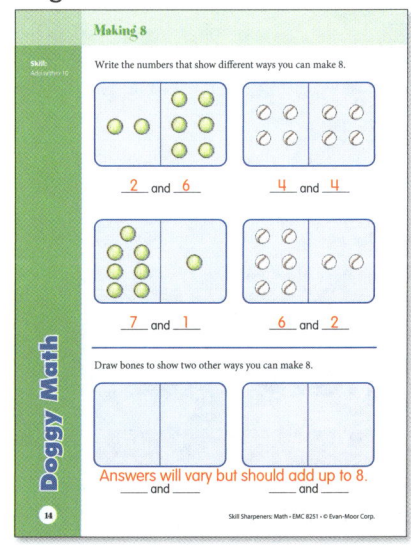

Page 15
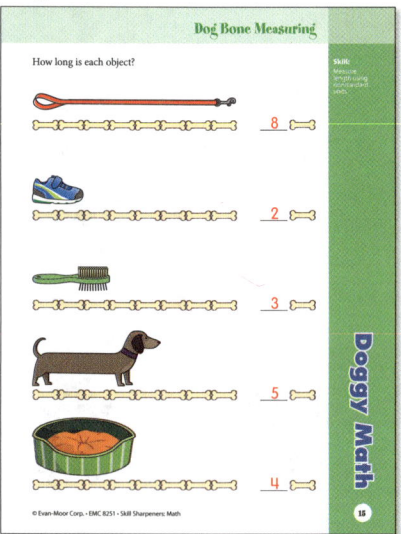

Page 16
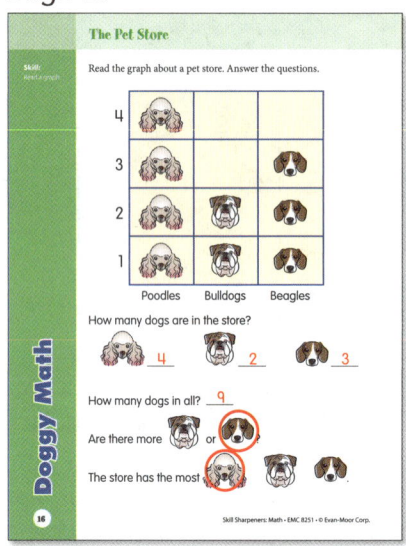

Page 17
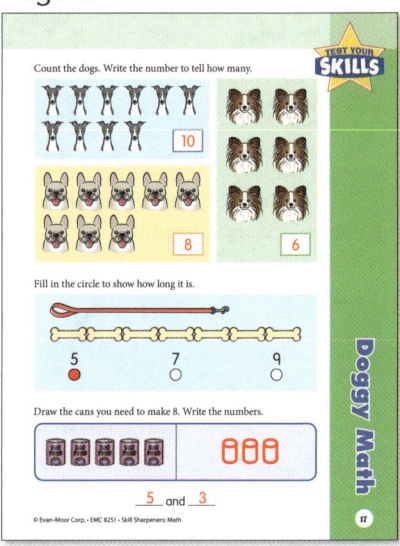

Page 18
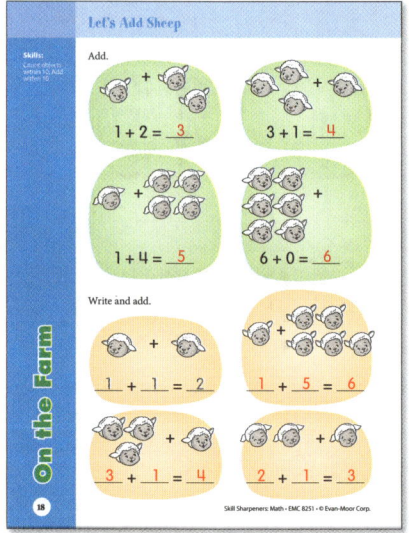

Page 19

Page 20

Page 21

Page 22

Page 23

Page 24

Page 25
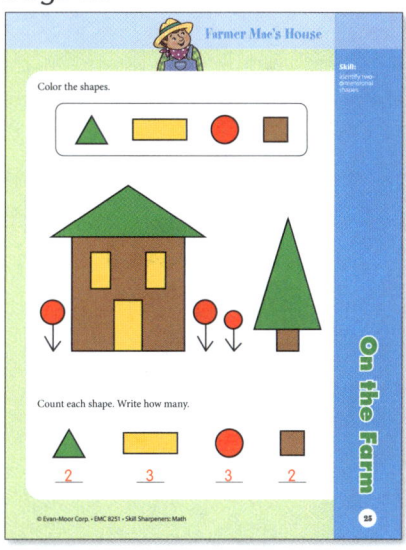

Page 26
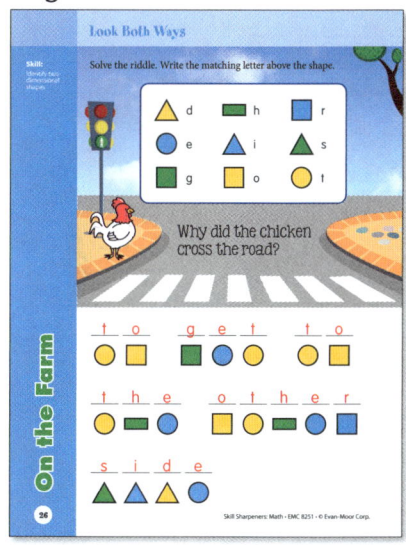

Page 27

Page 28
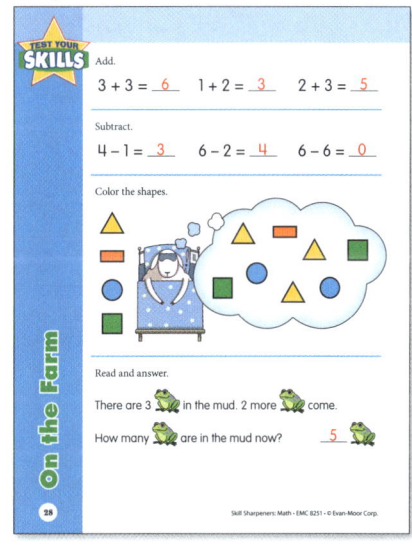

Page 29
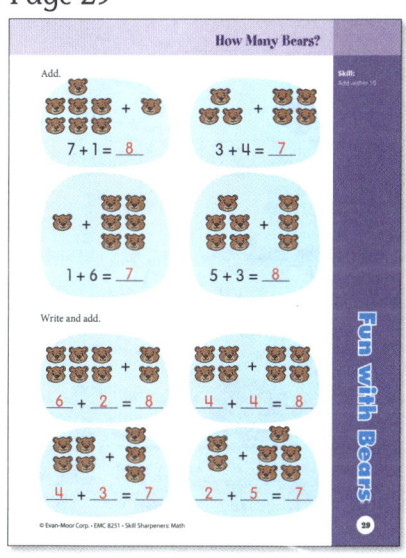

Page 30
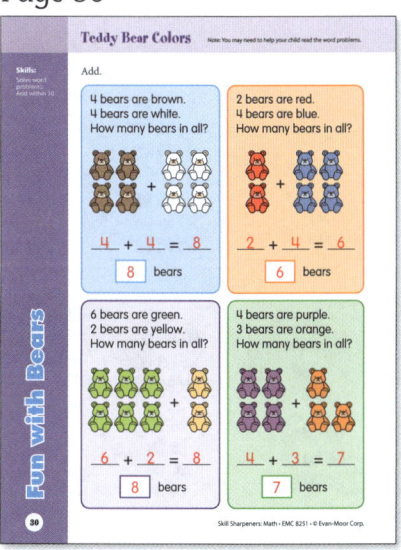

Page 31

Page 32
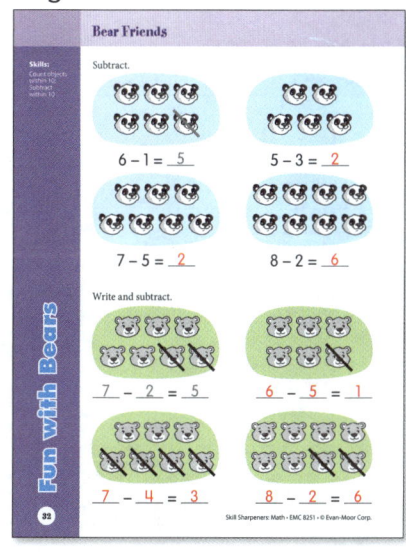

Page 33

Page 34

Page 35

Page 36
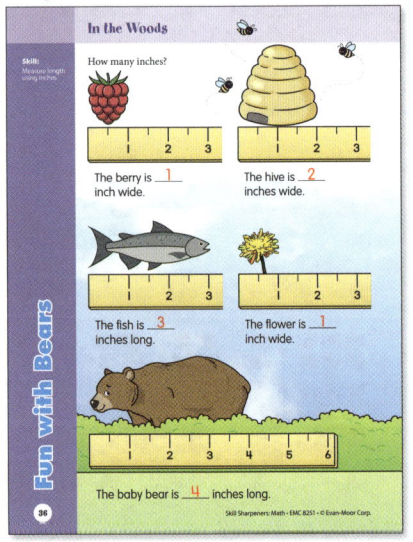

Page 37

Page 38
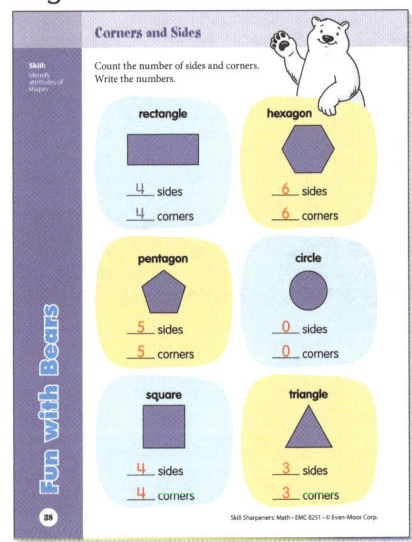

Page 39
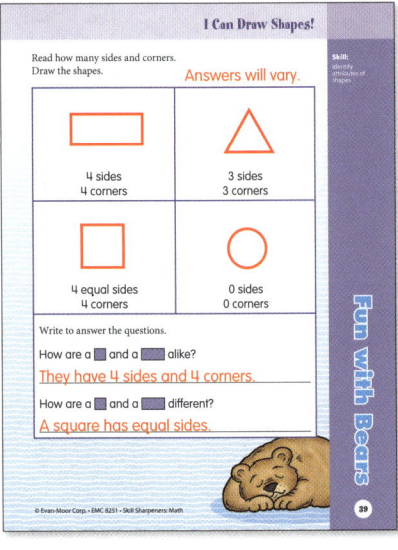

Page 40
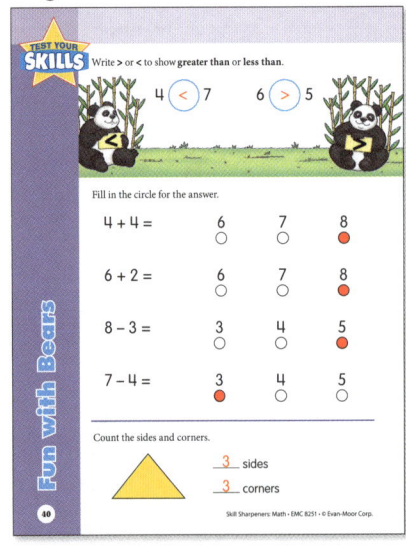

Page 41
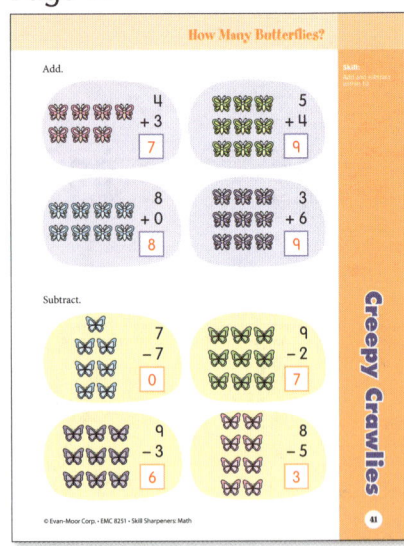

Page 42
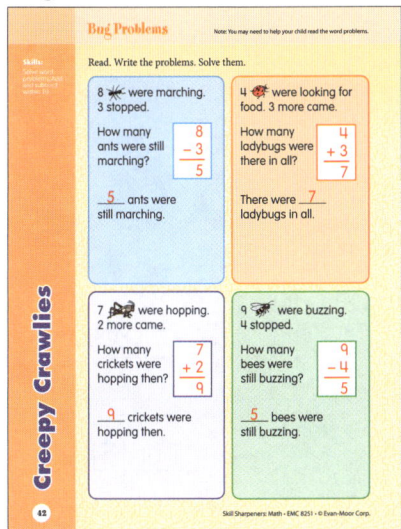

Page 43
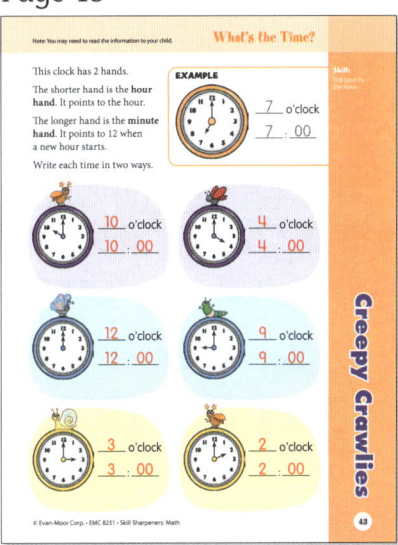

Page 44
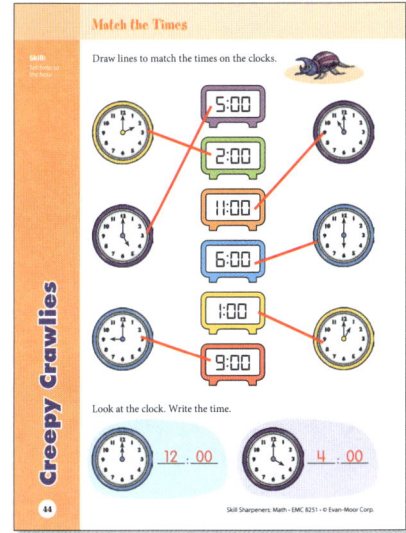

Page 45
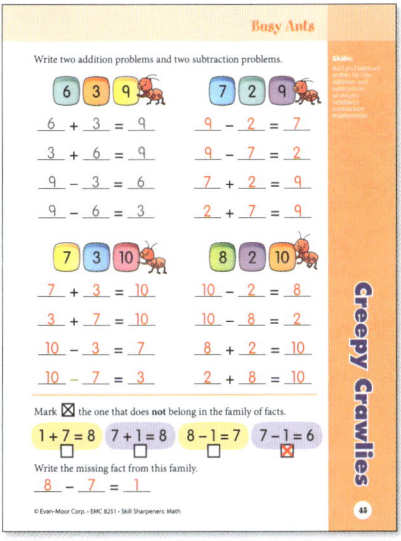

Page 46

Page 47
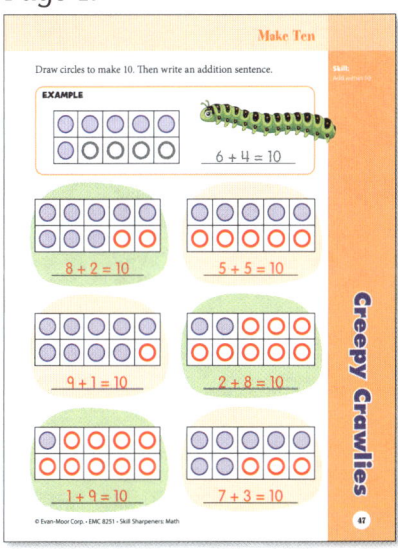

Page 48
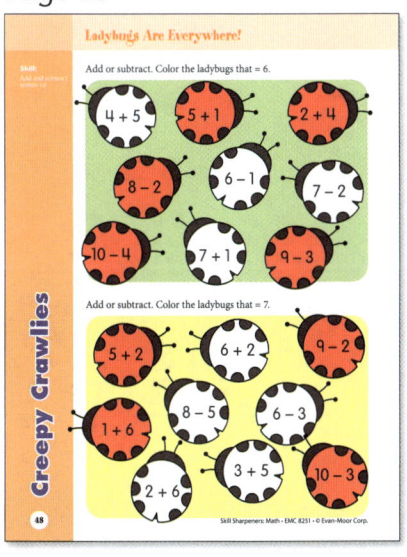

Page 49
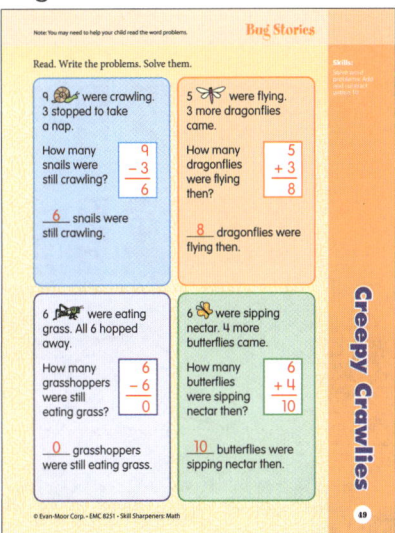

Page 50
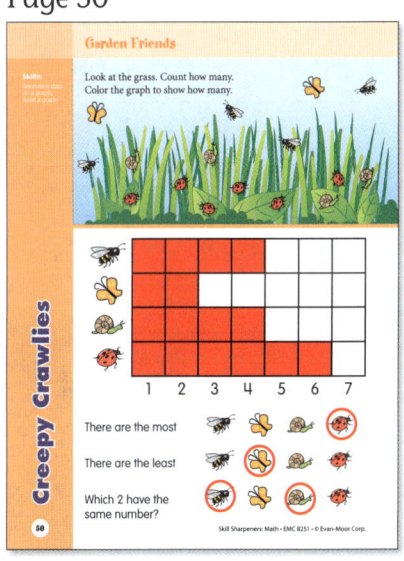

© Evan-Moor Corp. • EMC 8251 • Skill Sharpeners: Math

Page 51

Page 52

Page 53
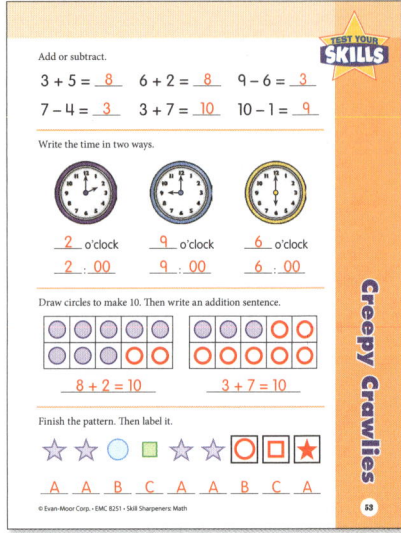

Page 54
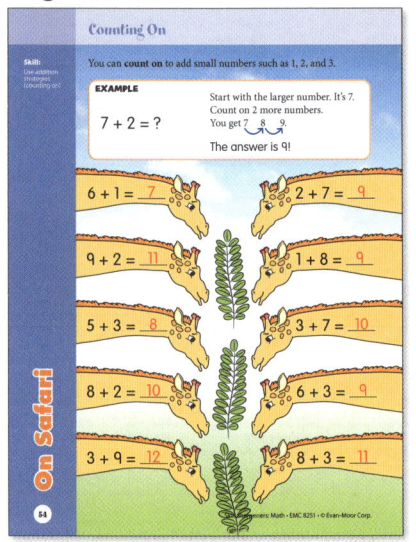

Page 55

Page 56

Page 57

Page 58

Page 59
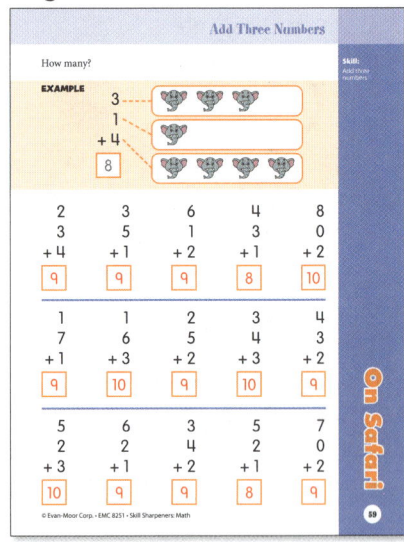

Page 60

Page 61
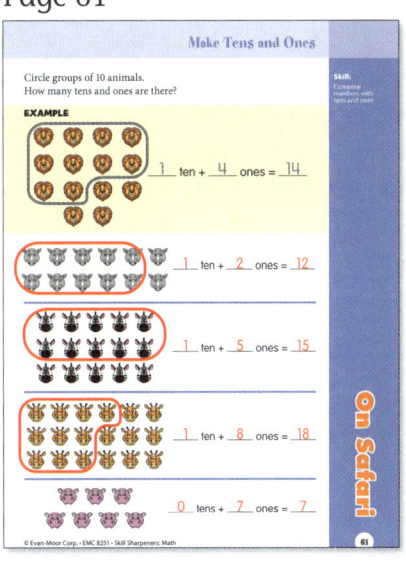

Page 62

Page 63
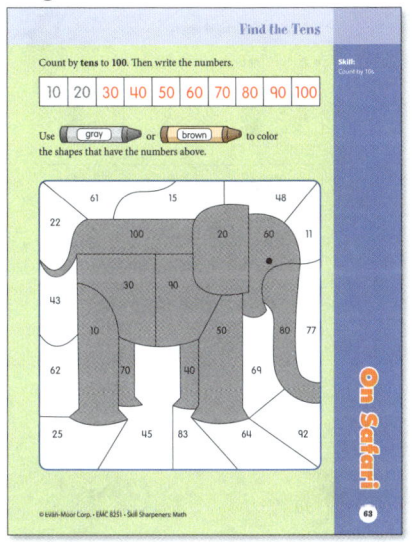

Page 64

Page 65

Page 66
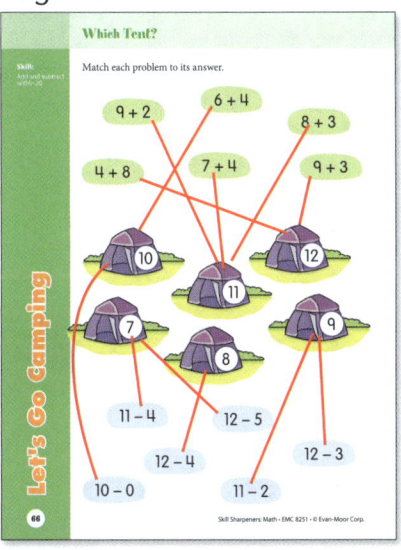

Page 67

Page 68
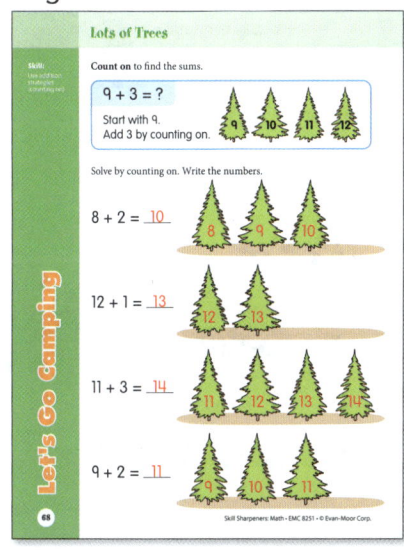

Page 69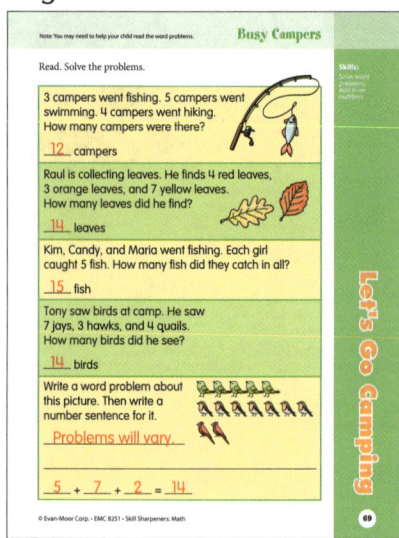

Page 70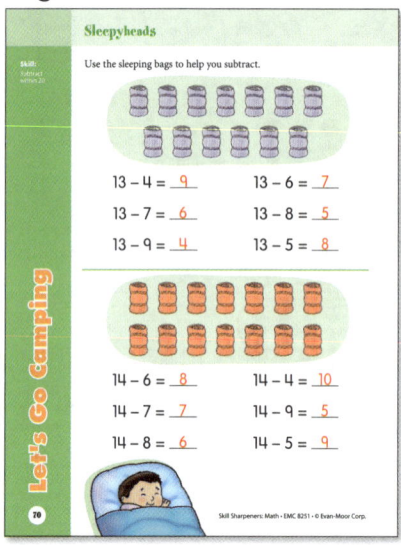

Page 71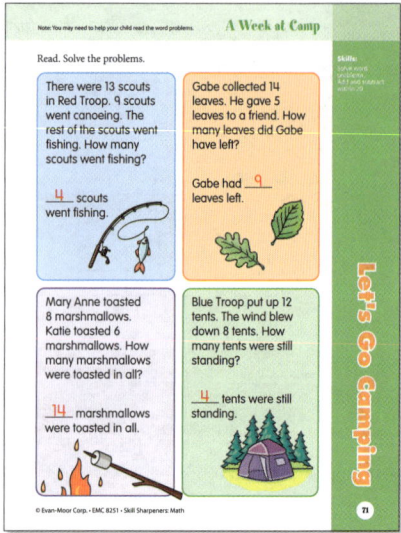

Page 72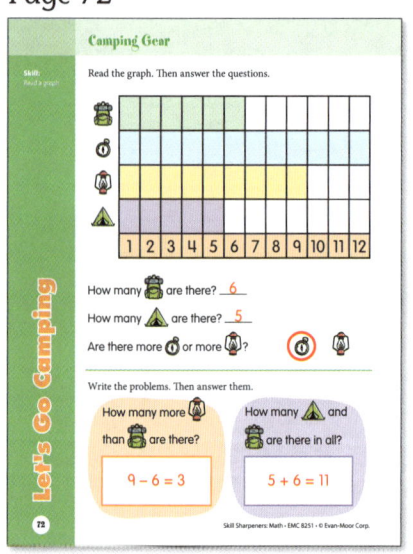

Page 73

Page 74

Page 75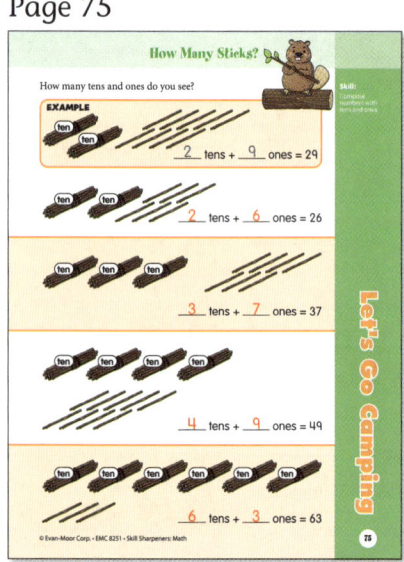

Page 76

Page 77

Page 78
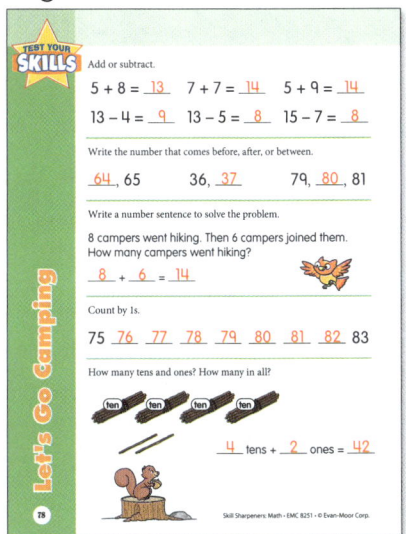

Page 79

Page 80

Page 81

Page 82
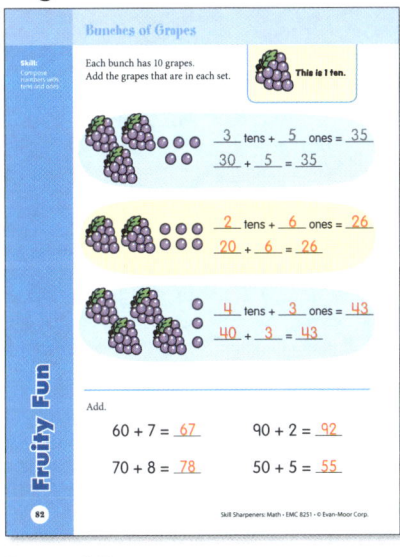

Page 83

Page 84
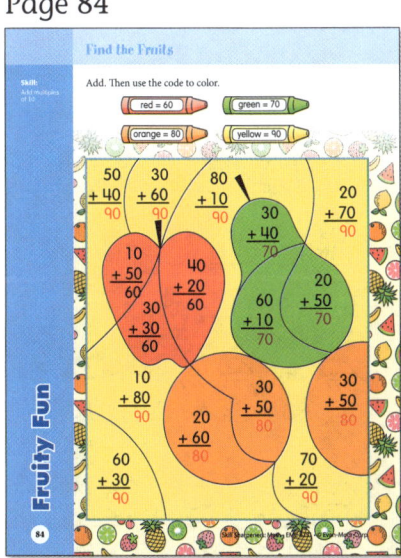

Page 85
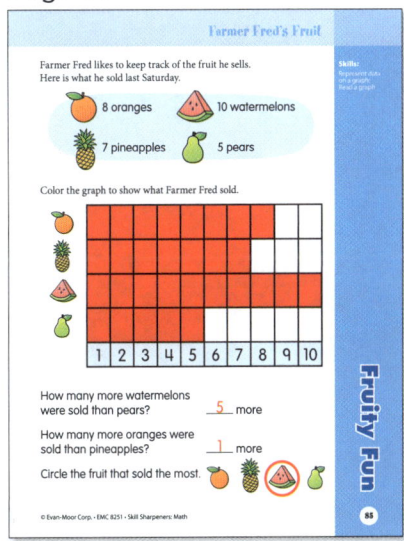

Page 86
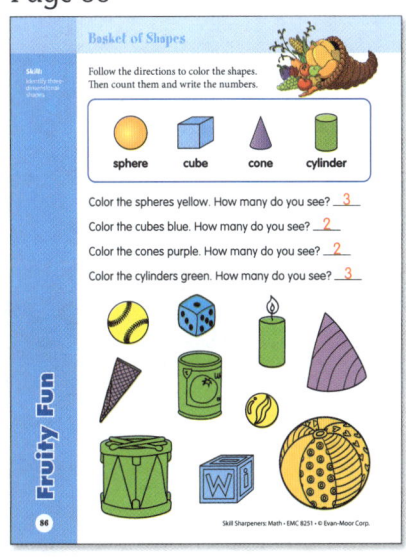

Page 87
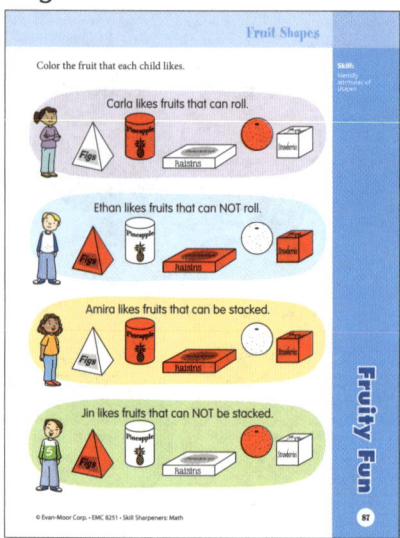

Page 88
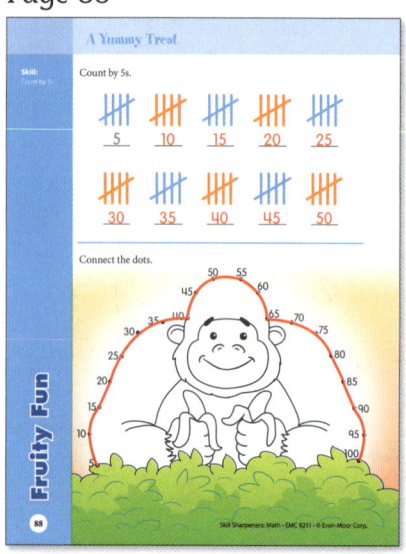

Page 89

Page 90

Page 91

Page 92

Page 93

Page 94

Page 95

Page 96
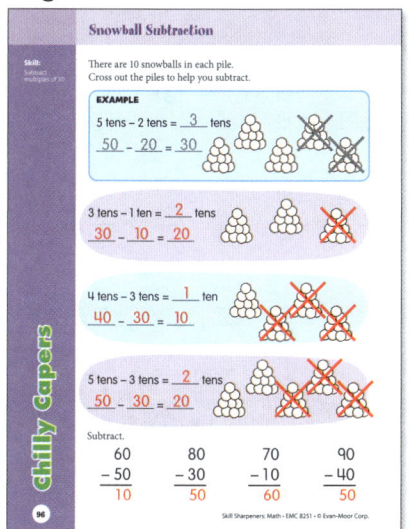

Page 97

Page 98

Page 99

Page 100
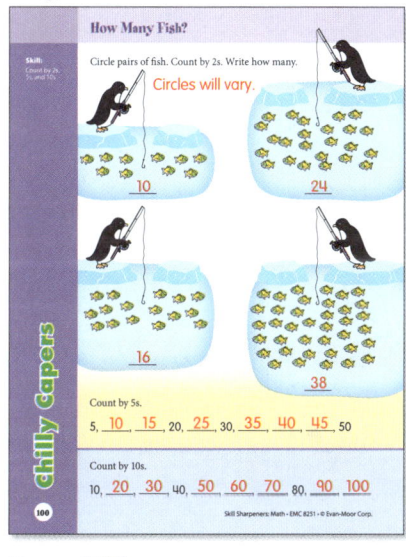

Page 101
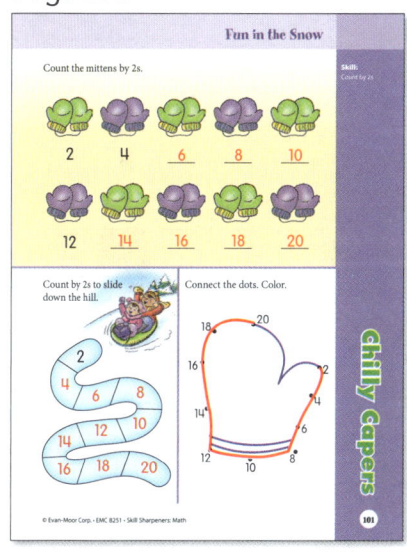

Page 102
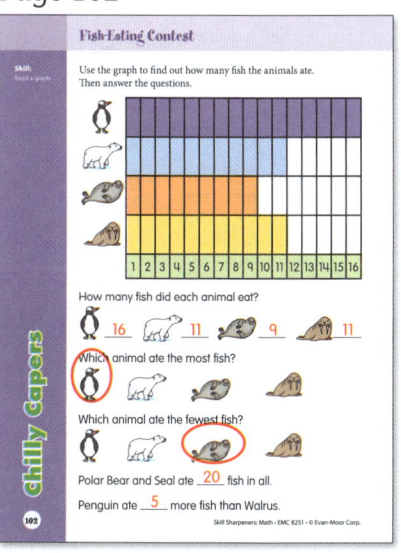

Page 103

Page 104

© Evan-Moor Corp. • EMC 8251 • Skill Sharpeners: Math

141

Page 105
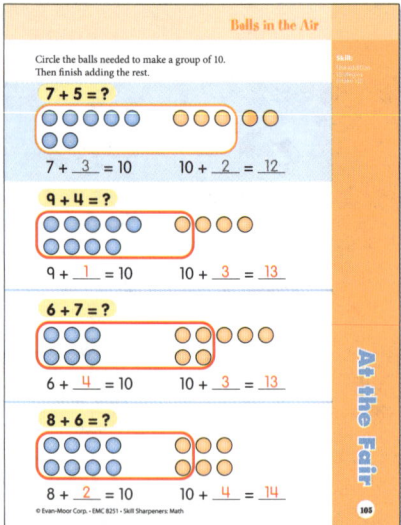

Page 106
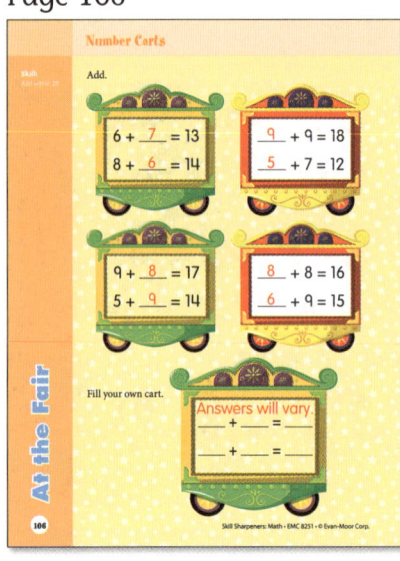

Page 107

Page 108

Page 109
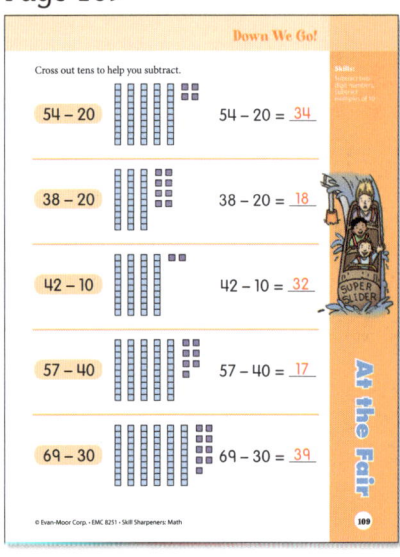

Page 110

Page 111
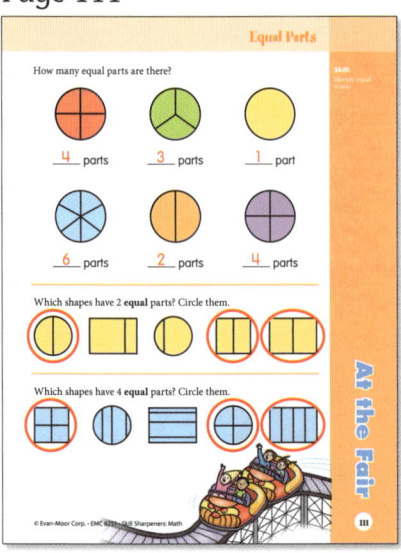

Page 112
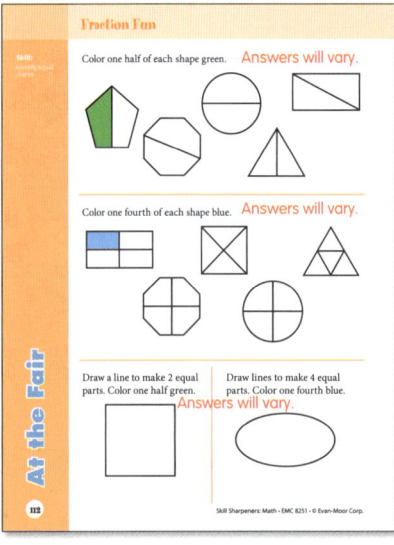

Page 113

Page 114
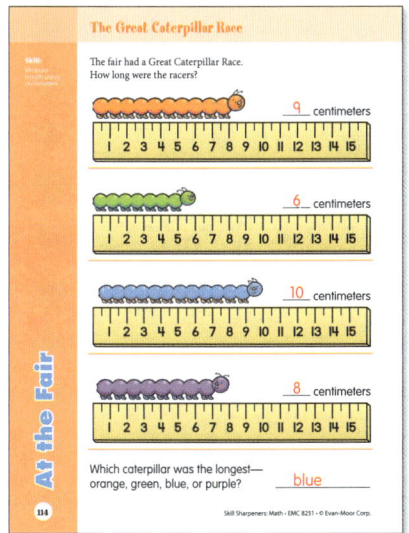

Page 115
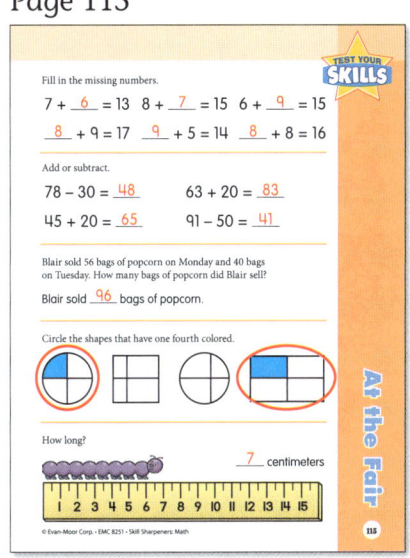

Page 116
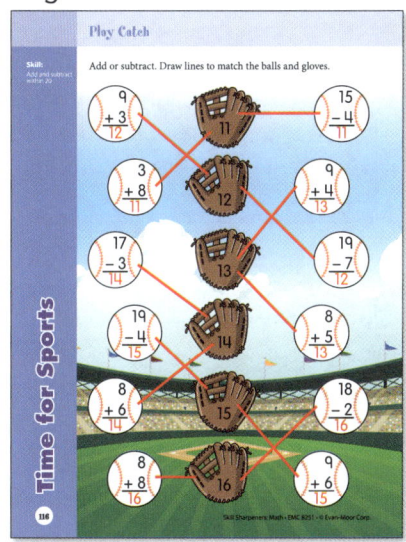

Page 117
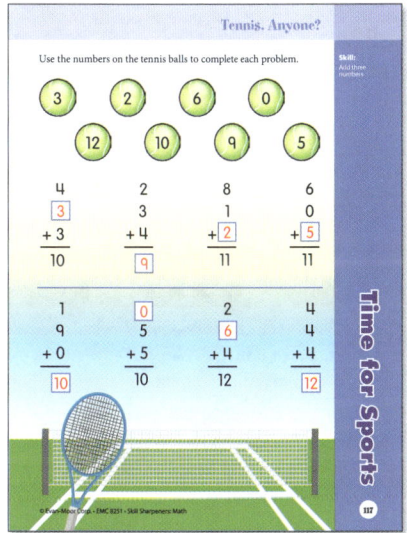

Page 118
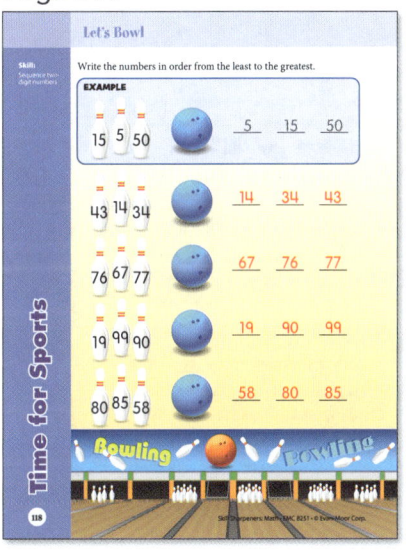

Page 119
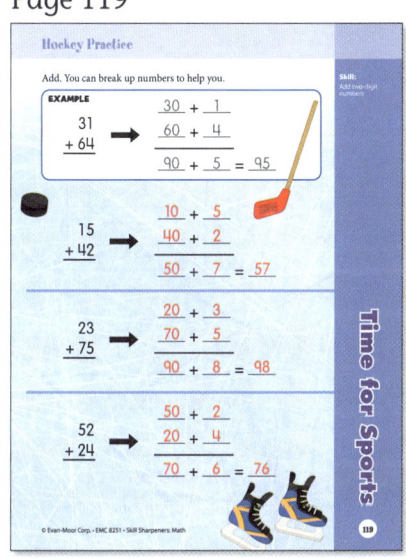

Page 120

Page 121
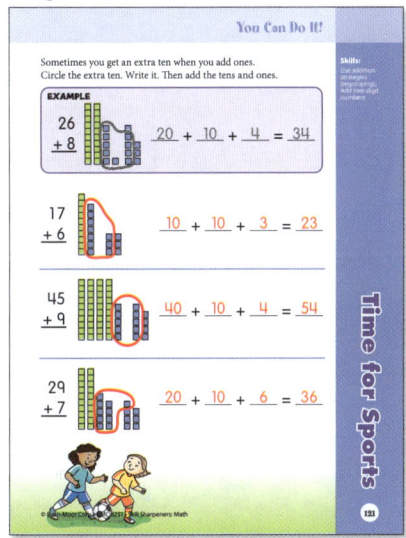

Page 122

Page 123

Page 124

Page 125

Page 126
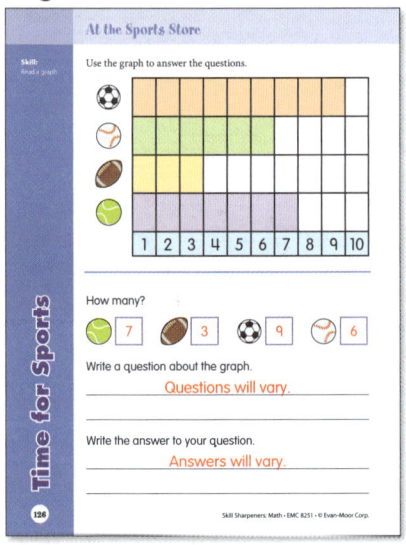

Page 127
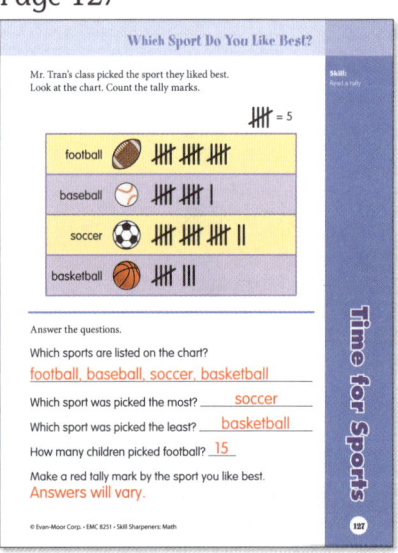

Page 128
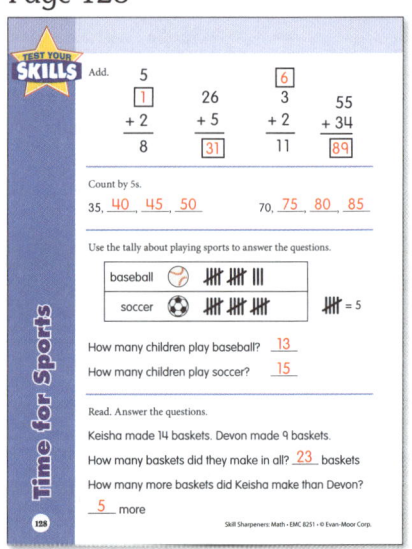